paperwork

paperwork

**the potential of paper in
graphic design**

written by
nancy williams
designed by
williams and phoa

Phaidon Press Limited
Regent's Wharf
All Saints Street
London N1 9PA

Phaidon Press Inc.
180 Varick Street
New York
NY 10014

www.phaidon.com

First published 1993
Reprinted 1994
Reprinted in paperback 1995,
1997, 2001
© 1993 Phaidon Press Limited
Text © 1993 Nancy Williams

ISBN 0 7148 3461 0

A CIP catalogue record for
this book is available from
the British Library

Printed in China

contents **paperwork**

author's note

Pages **61** and **95** have been die-stamped and creased. Readers are invited to hand-finish these pages by manipulating or cutting and folding as appropriate

7 **introduction**

11 **paper qualities**

33 **surface effects**

61 **manipulation**

95 **three dimensions**

113 **alternative materials**

129 **mixed media**

152 **terms and techniques**

159 **index**

Because of its ubiquity, paper is often taken for granted - even by designers. This book is therefore long overdue. It is intended, through international examples, to inspire all those who use paper - from designers to printers and merchants - to encourage them to experiment and to extend their boundaries by trying printing materials and applications that they may not have considered before. While this is not a manual - there are no instructions - every effort has been made to give as much technical detail and guidance as possible. There is also a section at the back of the book which should answer most questions regarding the properties and limitations of different types of materials and their suitability for various printing and finishing effects.

The first sheets of paper were made in China in about 200 BC; since then it has become indispensable. Paper was originally intended to be purely a carrier of images and scripts, but because of its natural properties - strength, flexibility and durability - and its low costs, it has subsequently been developed and exploited to produce a vast variety of items from disposable clothing to loudspeaker cones. However, the main use of paper continues to be as a surface on which to record information.

In recent years there has been an encouraging increase in experimentation with different sorts of papers and in the diversity of techniques, both traditional and new, which designers apply to them. Whereas in the past there may have been some resistance to this, both printers and manufacturers are now becoming increasingly accommodating. The result has been work achieved because of the combined expertise of all concerned, and there is no substitute for in-depth discussion between the various trades to ensure that every avenue is explored while physical limitations are acknowledged.

For designers, choosing the right paper for a job should be just as important as choosing the right typeface - both decisions are part of the designer's creative input. However tight the brief, however demanding or restricting the client, the choice of paper is generally the designers. I feel that time spent finding the perfect stock for the job is personally very rewarding because of the enhanced quality of the resulting project and the satisfaction of a job well done. However important the concept of a design, the execution is often what determines its success, and at williams and phoa we pride ourselves in getting the details right - be it in typography, colour or paper. Perfection may not be attainable, but it is well worth striving for.

Sometimes, though, it is just not possible to get the paper you want; many are made for specialist industrial uses and it can be difficult to track them down or to have them made available for other purposes. The production of this book was a case in point. We have not used any unusual papers for the text pages - they are printed on a standard stock which is particularly suitable for books. However, we had wanted it to have a protective wrapping made of a particular silicone-covered paper which is found on the back of tracing pads. Unfortunately this proved impossible to obtain.

However, on other occasions perseverance pays off. Many paper mills will, for instance, make batches of paper in odd weights or sizes, if a large enough quantity is ordered. In the case of something like an annual report, reducing the weight by a few grams could save a lot of money both on the paper and on postage. Sheet size, too, can have economic implications: if the only available sizes are inappropriate for the design, the wastage can be so great that a fundamentally inexpensive stock can prove uneconomical.

The speed at which paper mills reacted to the pressure of environmental issues to review their methods and sources of pulp is an indication of their current adaptability and willingness to respond to designers' requests. The outcome of this has been a dramatic increase in the range of papers available. It is also encouraging to see the resurgence in popularity of old crafts and skills including paper-making and letterpress printing. Add to these the more modern effects such as laser-cutting, and designers have a wider choice of both papers and methods of manipulating them than ever before.

Nevertheless many designers steer clear of experimenting with anything out of the ordinary and fail to venture further than a very limited range of papers and run-of-the-mill techniques. It is, of course, a trap which we all fall into now and again. But, as the illustrations in this book show, those who are open-minded in their approach to one aspect of design tend to be receptive to all sorts of influences and ideas and do not impose artificial parameters on what they can and cannot do. Consequently, some names recur in these pages as producers of innovative work, and their designs will be found scattered throughout the book because of their imaginative uses of many techniques - binding, folding, cutting, embossing and so on.

For the sake of clarity the book has been divided into six sections. Each one focuses on a particular aspect of design or range of techniques from paper qualities and surface effects to mixed media. However, although sometimes a piece of work was notable for only one aspect of its design, in many cases the decision as to which section a piece should go in had to be rather arbitrary. In fact, some of the most exciting work which we came across was impressive precisely because of its innovative use of a number of different techniques and materials, and could have been included in several sections. And not only was some of the work difficult to categorize; so were some of the techniques which we look at: embossing, for instance, has been treated as a surface effect, although it could just as well have been in the section about manipulation, whereas binding has been categorized as manipulation, although not everyone would expect to find it there.

Some other points should be made about the selection of work for this volume. First, the choice has been arrived at from submissions received and research undertaken in many parts of the world, as far afield as Japan and the USA. Indeed, work from Japan alone could probably have filled an entire book. Inevitably, therefore, many excellent examples have had to be omitted in the interest of variety and clarity of presentation.

Second, the work which has been included might not necessarily be considered outstanding in every respect: some pieces are primarily interesting examples of a particular technique or approach. However, all the projects shown, in one way or another, illustrate what can be achieved by designers who do not take their basic materials and craft skills for granted.

paper qualities **paperwork**

12   techniques

paper qualities

paper as artwork

graphic recycled

Choosing exactly the right paper can be what makes the difference between a good and an exquisite job. The sheen, texture, colour and weight of the stock can all enhance, transform or even dictate the design. The tactile qualities of paper can be used in an expressive way: the dull surface of an uncoated paper could suggest sober sophistication in a bank's annual report; a high-gloss art paper can literally add gloss to a fashion retailer's brochure.

It is, however, easy to fall into the habit of specifying the same few tried and tested papers over and over again, knowing that the results will be good, but missing the chance to create something stunning. Paper, like colour, typography and design itself, is subject to fashion. Often the stock or type of stock which first springs to mind as appropriate for a job is just the one which is currently most popular. Nevertheless, as we have said, designers are becoming more adventurous, specifying papers which have not generally been used before, or using familiar papers in imaginative ways. Printers, too, are becoming more open to experimentation.

Unusual papers are not necessarily prohibitively expensive. Many, however, are highly priced because they are shipped from abroad or produced in a labour-intensive way. Japanese papers, in particular, tend to be expensive but they can be so beautiful that it is well worth considering how their use could enhance a job if the budget allows. Nevertheless, there are various unusual papers which look expensive but in fact are not - it is always worth checking the price before assuming that a particularly attractive paper would cost too much. There is, for instance, a seemingly extravagant hand-made paper, Inclusion Florale, produced at the Richard de Bas Mill in France, which has freshly-gathered flowers incorporated into the pulp, but is surprisingly reasonable.

The production of such hand-made papers is undergoing a renaissance, and for small commercial runs with adequate time in their schedules it is sometimes feasible to have them customized for specific needs. Flowers, pieces of ephemera or specially designed elements can be added to the stock, or alternatively specially created watermarks can be incorporated into the paper, perhaps strategically placed to suit the design. The Christmas card made for Brian Delaney Associates on page 29, uses a specially hand-made paper which incorporates pieces of the previous year's cards in an effective example of graphic recycling.

As well as being used as part of the structure of a design, paper can be turned into artwork, to be reproduced as an alternative to a more traditional form of illustration such as photography, drawing or painting. Graphic designers seeking to extend their means of expression will often turn to paper, a medium with which they are obviously very familiar, and use it to illustrate their print work. Among the visual clichés which will no doubt continue to be used because of their simplicity and immediate communicative effect are screwed-up paper, paper aeroplanes and darts, and slashes and tears in paper.

Graphic recycling - the mixture of bits and pieces of old paper, print and ephemera to create new artworks - is also popular with many designers and illustrators. The juxtapositions possible with this sort of collage can be very expressive, ranging from the humorous to the sinister, as images and textures with very different associations are mixed on the printed page or surface.

The following examples include work using machine-made, mould-made and hand-made papers, papers which were specially made for the project in question - some of the Japanese work is particularly exciting and inspirational. For most jobs though, commissioning a special stock, or making it in-house, will be out of the question. Nevertheless, the extra time spent finding a standard stock with exactly the right qualities, smooth or textured, matt or gloss, will be well rewarded.

Recycling

Despite the recent surge of interest in recycling, there are still few designers who exploit recycled paper's natural tone and texture and use them excitingly as positive features of their design - evidenced by the fact that recycling does not have a section of its own. Very often the recycled stock chosen is so smooth and white as to be virtually indistinguishable from some virgin paper - and sometimes it is not as environmentally friendly as its 'recycled' label would imply.

Recycled paper will not be the right choice for every job; the pros and cons of using it need to be considered beforehand. In its favour, of course, are the environmental advantages, although these vary considerably depending on how the paper was made and what went into it. Generally speaking, however, any recycled paper is better for the environment than a virgin stock because recycling causes less pollution than making virgin paper, and it helps mitigate the increasingly pressing problem of how to dispose of all the waste paper we create. Also, paper which is self-evidently recycled signals a client's concern for the environment very clearly. In addition, it can give a natural, honest look to the work.

When choosing a recycled stock for environmental reasons, the following points should always be considered. First, what proportion of the paper is recycled? Usually some virgin stock is added to the recycled pulp for increased strength, but this proportion varies from stock to stock.

Second, what was the recycled element made from? In some papers it is just 'millbroke', the clean offcuts from the virgin paper-making process. More environmentally friendly papers use pulp from 'post-consumer waste', paper which has already been used. As a rule of thumb, paper made from post-consumer waste is unusually greyish and flecked with ink particles, although this is not so if the pulp has been cleaned. Third, if the paper is chlorine-bleached, this process creates long-lasting toxic effluents; hydrogen peroxide-bleaching is considered to be less harmful, but unbleached paper is best of all.

The various factors affect whether the paper is defined as recycled or environmentally friendly. Much heated debate continues over which of these is in fact more considerate of the environment.

The drawbacks of recycled paper are that it is never as white as virgin stock and that it tends to absorb the ink much more, leading to dot gain. To get the best from it, these factors should be considered from the start of the design process: half-tones and tints, for instance, may have to be adjusted or avoided, along with very small type which may be difficult to read against an off-white or flecked background, especially once it has 'bled'. However, some of the new 'environmentally friendly' papers that have been released into the market are exceptional and print just as well as standard stocks.

A common misconception is that recycled paper is bound to be cheaper than virgin paper; however the reverse is often true. So before specifying, it is always best to check.

Designers who work with recycled paper rather than trying to disguise it can produce results which are just as aesthetically sophisticated as anything done with virgin paper. Its muted tones and interesting textures can become the highlight of a design if, for instance, they are combined with inks of similarly subtle shades, or maybe contrasted with a luminous ink. There is, of course, no reason why recycled and virgin papers should not be mixed in the same piece of work. For something such as an annual report, in which different sections need to be easily identified, using a recycled stock for one part and a contrasting virgin stock in another could be ideal. Other interesting contrasts can be achieved by foil blocking recycled stock: the smooth shine of the metal against the rough surface of the paper can give an unusual feel to the work. However, it should be borne in mind that paper which has been foil blocked or varnished cannot then be recycled and so for clients who are using recycled paper for environmental reasons these techniques should perhaps be avoided.

16 Interesting designs do not necessarily require exotic materials: this information pack for the UK's Design and Art Direction organization's student awards has illustrations made from ordinary brown paper envelopes, an idea inspired by the fact that the awards were sponsored by the British Royal Mail. By cutting and folding, the envelopes have been made to suggest a number of themes, from magazine design to copy writing. The cover of the information pack has an envelope which has been folded to look like a pencil - the D&AD's symbol - creating a visual link between D&AD and the Royal Mail.

designed by
Carter Wong, London
designers
Philip Carter, Philip Wong
art director
Philip Carter
client
Design and Art Direction

The initials of this firm of architects were created out of folded paper, its sculptural look conveying the three-dimensional nature of their work. The paper artwork was photographed for reproduction on the firm's letterhead, and the theme was continued on a poster, the folded paper representing the head and shoulders of a messenger.

designed by
williams and phoa, London
designer
Phoa Kia Boon
client
Nicholas Gill Associates
stock
**letterhead: Mellotex matt
ultra white 155gsm
poster: Parilux matt 200gsm**

18 The multi-layered appearance of
the type and images in this
Apple Mac-generated design
has been emphasized by
printing some of the pages on
translucent paper so that the
type shows through to the
reverse side and overlays the
images behind it. The book,
called *From the Edge*, illustrates
work by architecture and design
students.

designed by
**April Greiman Incorporated,
California**
designers
April Greiman, Sean Adams
client
**Southern California Institute
of Architecture**

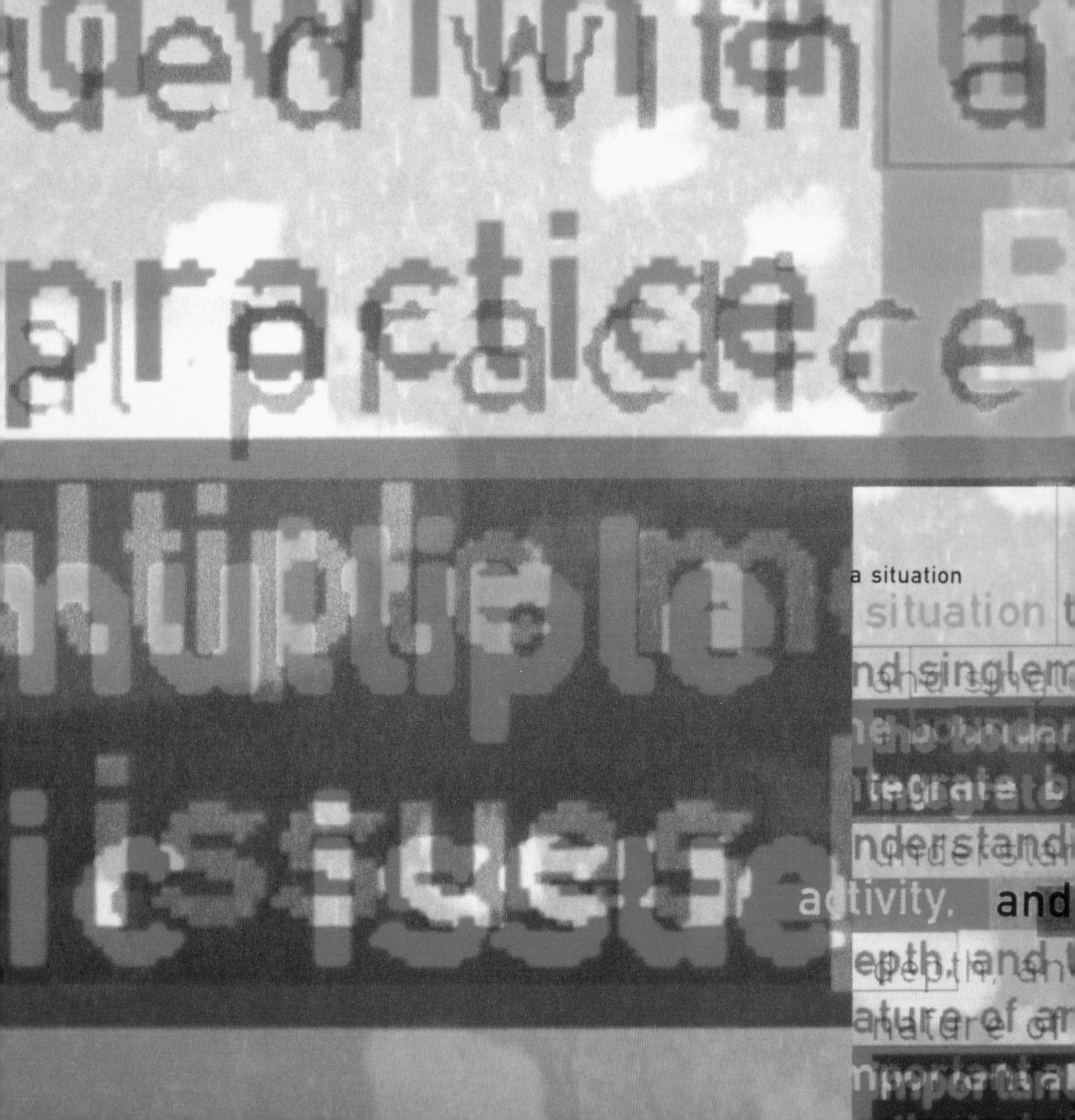

...ued with a

practice s

...ultiple m

...is tructe

a situation
...situation t
...and single m
...method...
...integrate b
...understand
activity, and
...epth, and t
...ature of an
...important

20   Designed to be easily updated, this furniture company's price list consists of an opaque inner leaflet containing product information, with a transluscent wrap-around cover on which the prices are printed.

designed by
Lippa Pearce, London
designer
Harry Pearce
art directors
Harry Pearce, Domenic Lippa
client
Humber Contract Furniture
printer
Vitesse Printing
stock
wraparound: Zanders T2000 RO 145-155gsm
inner: Consort Royal Silk tint 170gsm

Tracing paper has been used as a metaphor in this brochure: the designers say they wanted the layered effect of the paper to mirror what they describe as the 'many-layered skills' of the client, an interior design company. With its tracing paper pages and opaque end-papers, it reverses an old graphic tradition.

designed by
Bull Rodger, London
designer
Jonathan Cook
art director
Paul Rodger
client
Allman Associates
stock
matt art paper 170gsm, Rives satin transparent 140gsm

paper qualities **paperwork**

22 The lightweight, semi-transparent stock used for this book has been bound together in French folds: each page comprises two layers of paper, creased at the edge. The inside surfaces of the paper have been printed and the resulting show-through of shadowy shapes, muted colours and type provides an intriguing semi-abstract background for the images and words printed on top of the pages.

designer
Jenni van Driel, Holland
printer
Drukkerij Rosbeek

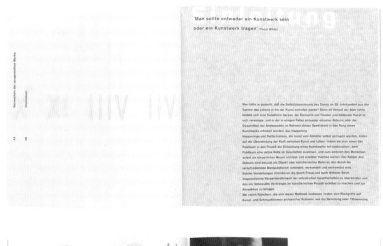

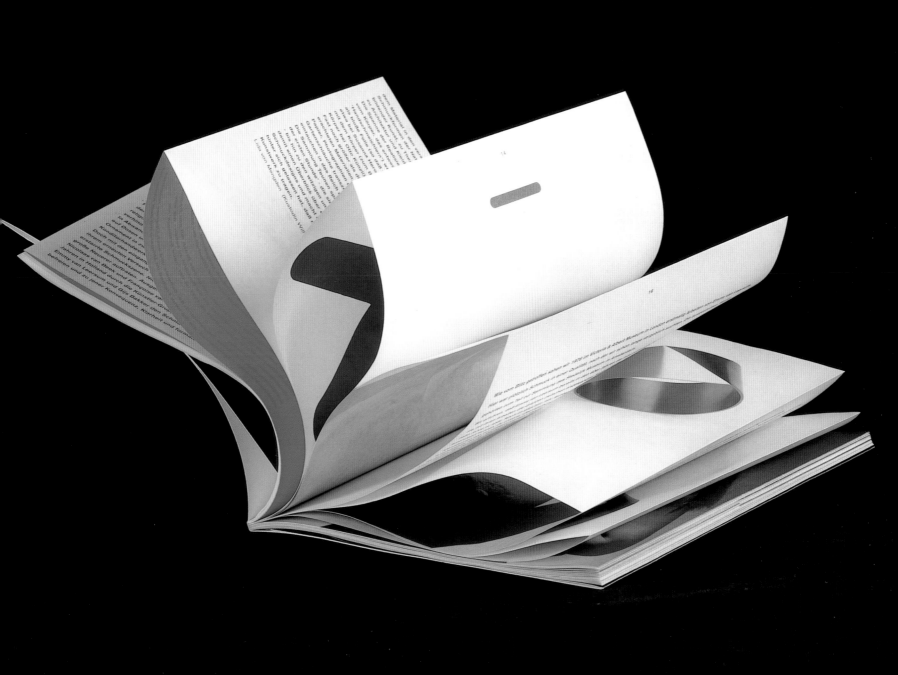

24 For this invitation, disguised to look like a 1920s photograph album, the designers wanted stocks which enhanced the illusion of antiquity. The inside pages of rough card were die-cut to hold the photographs, and the cover deliberately printed to look worn.

designed by
N & N, London
designer
Mark Owen
art director
Romanus Odiwe
client
N & N
printer
First Impression
stock
**dust jacket: Wiggins Teape Speckletone 104gsm
cover: Speckletone 216gsm
pages: Keaykolour 150gsm**

Based on the four seasons, this lavish portfolio of limited edition prints was designed as a present for people attending the Royal Gala opening night at London's Chelsea Flower Show. Covered in a hand-made paper embedded with leaves and flowers, and fastened with a ribbon, the portfolio was intended to be something which people would want to keep. Inside, the prints were tipped-in to a blind embossed page, letterpressed with the titles of the images which were then wrapped in lense tissue and sealed with special labels.

designed by
williams and phoa, London
designers
Nancy Williams
Laura Heard
client
Olympia and York
printer
litho: CTD
letterpress: Hand and Eye
binders
Studio Bindery
stock
cover: Inclusions Florales
prints: Rivoli 240gsm
mounts: Somerset White
Textured 300gsm
tissue: Lense tissue

26 An ordinary, inexpensive stock has been used to create a sophisticated range of stationery for fashion designer Koji Tatsuno. The solid red ink printed on the reverse of the paper bleeds through to create an unusual mottled effect.

designed by
Area, London
designers
Richard Smith, Cara Gallardo
art director
Yvonne Sporre
client
Koji Tatsuno
printer
Richard Harden Printing

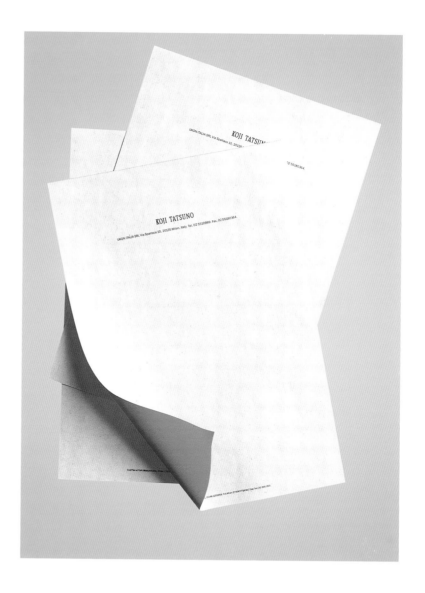

An envelope which is a good
example of the way in which the
unusual texture and natural
colour of a recycled stock can
be used to create a smart,
sophisticated design.

designed by
Akio Okumura, Japan
designer
Akio Okumura
client
Packaging Create
printer
Yaka Paper Manufacture

28 Embedded in the hand-made paper from which this Christmas card was made are a number of Norwegian Spruce tree seeds: recipients were instructed to plant the card and watch the trees grow. It is an idea which simultaneously alludes to recycling and Christmas trees, and is highly appropriate for the client, an environmental organization concerned for the future of West Africa's rain forests.

designed by
The Partners, London
designers
Keren House, David Kimpton
client
Earthlife
papermaker
David Stuart
printer
Royal College of Art
stock
pulp and bracken

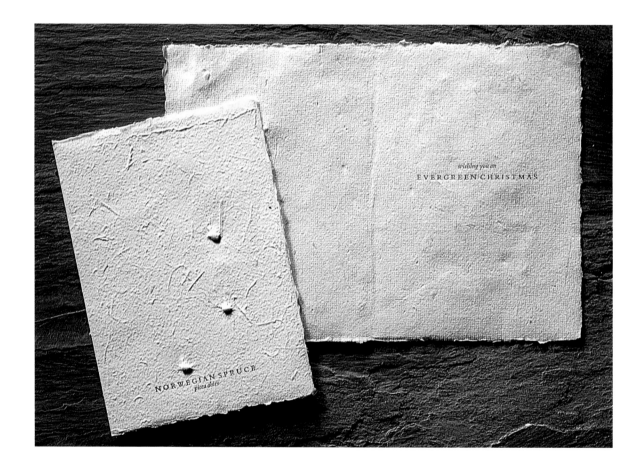

This is, quite literally, a recycled Christmas card. The designers tore up old cards and carefully added shreds of them to the pulp of the hand-made paper from which the new card was made, recycling both the paper and the graphics.

designed by
Brian Delaney Design Associates, London
designer
Jeff Willis
client
Brian Delaney Design Associates
manufacturer
Nautilus Press & Paper Mill
stock
hand-made from 100% cotton bedsheets and previous year's Christmas cards

30   The shapes which were die-cut from the cover of this calendar were collected by its designers and made into a model of a tree, reversing the usual progression from tree to paper. The resulting structure was a three-dimensional illustration of the theme of the calendar, chain reaction, which explored the way that one thing leads to another, with particular reference made to the environment. Underlining the theme, the whole calendar was printed on recycled stock.

designer
Trickett and Webb, London
client
Trickett and Webb/Augustus Martin
printer
Augustus Martin
stock
speckletone recycled paper and strawboard

chain reaction 1989 calendar published by trickett & webb and augustus martin

32   Unwanted sheets of printed
paper were gathered from
printers' floors and re-used in
this catalogue for an art
exhibition. The designers were
inspired to do this graphic
recycling by the gallery artists'
preoccupations with
deconstructing mass-produced
objects and putting them in new
contexts. The waste print was
overprinted, and collated with
text pages of recycled stock.

designed by
**Imagination Design and
Communication, London**
designers
Adrian Caddy, David Booth
client
Goldsmiths Gallery
printers
**Litho-tech, Indepth, Merlin
Reprographics**

surface effects **paperwork**

34 **techniques**

embossing

foil blocking

letterpress

offset litho

silkscreen

tipping-in

From scratch-and-sniff ink to foil blocking, the range of surface effects that can be achieved on paper is enormous. Many of them, however, seem to be neglected, for example embossing is seldom employed for anything other than type or company logos. Whatever the effect, however, it is important that the paper chosen is suitable: metallic ink printed on to matt paper, for instance, will look dull because the metallic particles sink into the surface of the paper and so are unable to reflect light well.

Offset litho, although the most common method of printing, can give surprising results. Luminous, fluorescent, thermally sensitive and scratch-and-sniff inks are all available, and many manufacturers will make up more unusual inks for particular jobs. Matt inks, for example, which have better covering qualities on matt paper, can be mixed at only a little extra cost. In general, providing ample time is available, experimentation with unusual inks is well worthwhile. Ordinary materials can be excitingly transformed, for example, a piece of seemingly plain paper will change colour the instant it is touched if it has been printed with thermal ink.

Letterpress, a technique undergoing a revival, is worth considering for smaller print runs. The distinctive bite of the type into the paper and the craft feel which it gives to the end result can make a good job look particularly special. Hand-made and mould-made papers tend to give the best results because they provide the greatest contrast in texture between the lettering and its background, and allow the type or 'fleurons' to sink firmly into the surface.

Silkscreen is ideal for large surface areas, and makes it possible to print on board, fabrics, plastics and other unusual and awkward materials which will not go through a litho press. It is an adaptable process, and the thick spread of the ink can give rise to interesting results such as smooth-looking ink surfaces directly on top of contrastingly rough paper.

Embossing - another traditional technique - is still used frequently, but its full potential is seldom explored. Embossed images are created by pressing paper between a male and female die. Strictly speaking, the term embossing only applies when the resulting image is proud of the front surface of the paper; the reverse, when the image appears sunk into the surface, is called debossing. (The rectangular areas sunk into book covers or paper to take book plates or prints are described as being plate marked.) There are two types of embossing die: the first is an acid-etched photographically-exposed plate which gives a fairly shallow impression, all at one level. The second, more expensive type, is hand-engraved, which means that the results are only limited by the skills of the engraver and the suitability of the paper.

Choosing the right paper for embossed work is very important if tearing is to be prevented and a reasonable depth achieved. It is the length of the fibres in paper, not necessarily its weight, that determines how deep an emboss it can take; consequently hand-made paper is particularly suitable because of its long, randomly distributed fibres. Embossing has its limitations, however; it does not show up when faxed or photocopied, and embossed stationery may be flattened if fed through a laser printer.

As with die-stamping the size of the dies is generally restricted to A4. However, we have managed to track down one finisher in Scotland who was able to emboss up to A2.

Die-stamping, a similar technique, is usually only thought of for such traditional symbols as coats of arms and for company logos, but there is no reason why it should not be used in more exciting ways. Being a combination of embossing and gloss or matt coating, die-stamping tends to work best on matt uncoated papers. That aside, the only drawbacks with it are that it can require long lead times, and is subject to size restrictions. However, the accuracy and detail that can be achieved with die-stamping are phenomenal, making it very rewarding.

A less expensive alternative to die-stamping is thermography. This technique uses a thickness of resin to imitate the embossing and the gloss effect of die-stamping. Though once again this tends to be used on logos, I have seen interesting examples of covers using a combination of clear thermography and matt lamination

Despite the improvement of metallic inks, the only way to achieve a shiny, truly metallic look on paper is foil blocking. It can also be combined with embossing to provide a richer effect. Foils come in a variety of standard finishes, matt, gloss and metallic, as well as more unusual ones from mother of pearl to wood grain. Although not as expensive as some designers believe, once again there is a limit to the size of the area which can be blocked and sometimes to the length of print run possible, although, of course, several blocks could be used.

However strange or subtle the surface effect wanted, designers should not take no for an answer. If the first supplier approached cannot help, perseverance often pays off.

Designed to look as though a real wax seal has been applied to the page, the logo on this stationery is in fact an elaborate trompe l'oeil. The result of a large number of manipulation techniques, the seal was designed on an Apple Mac, hand-engraved in silver, proofed in black wax and photographed. It was then printed in full colour, ultra-violet-varnished and embossed.

designed by
Bull Rodger, London
designers
Paul Rodger, Laurence Grinter, Jonathan Cook
illustrator
Sue Sharples
engraver
John Snape
photography
Paul Bradforth
art direction
Paul Rodger
client
Paragon Vintners

38 A personal project by a
Japanese designer, the thick
paper used for this poster was
made using an old-fashioned
method. Layers of traditional
Japanese paper were apparently
pasted together, then covered
with a top sheet of Western
paper to achieve the white
surface; the result was
embossed and screen printed.

designed by
Kazumasa Nagai, Japan

A combination of heavy
embossing and luminous ink
gives this otherwise simple
stationery a vivid, three-
dimensional look.

designed by
**M Plus M Incorporated,
New York**
designer
Takaaki Matsumoto
art directors
**Takaaki Matsumoto,
Michael McGinn**
client
Pen Plus Inc
printer
Continental Bournique

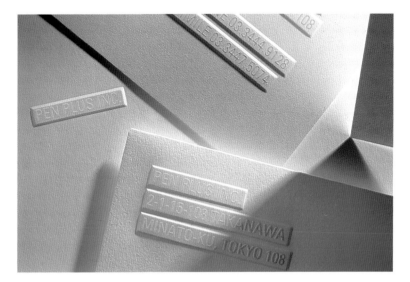

40   On the cover of this brochure, designed for British Rail's in-house department of architecture and design, blind embossing at two levels has been used to create a pattern of railway tracks. The theme has been continued inside, where careful cropping of the pictures and unusually angled captions hint at criss-crossing rails.

designed by
Roundel Design Group, London
designers
Michael Denny, John Bateson, Chris Bradley
client
British Rail, Department of Architecture and Design
printer
Mapledon Press

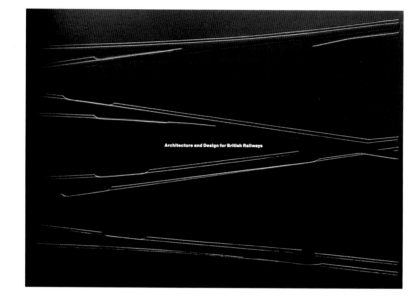

The blind embossing on the cover of this brochure mimics the anti-slip pattern on the metal flooring of train footplates. The brochure was designed for a consortium of design, architecture and engineering companies which work for transport-related industries; the pattern would be familiar to its readers.

design
Roundel Design Group, London
designers
Michael Denny, John Bateson, Chris Bradley, Rachael Dinnis
client
Transport Design Consortium
stock
cover: Parilux gloss 300gsm
text: Parilux matt 170gsm
printer
Fulmar Colour Printing

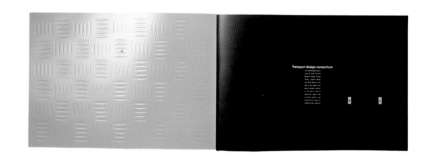

42 In this range of personal stationery, the business card has a dual role: when inserted into the die-cut slits in the paper it becomes the letterheading. The smoothness of the card stands out against the textured paper; two blind embossed circles mark the place where the card is inserted and look as though they are holding it on to the page.

designed by
williams and phoa, London
designer
Phoa Kia Boon
client
Charles Osborne
stock
card: Ivorex smooth
paper: Zeta matt

Although no ink has been printed on this calendar, its designers have differentiated Sundays and holidays from the rest of the week by using a mixture of blind embossing and debossing to create contrasting type.

designed by
Akio Okumura, Japan
designer
Makoto Ito
art director
Akio Okumura
client
Packaging Create Inc
printer
Fuji Paper Enterprise Association

44 The random fibres of this hand-made paper allow for a very deep impression, a property which has been exploited to the full in this calendar. The thickness of the paper and the depth of the debossing and embossing give it a three-dimensionality which, combined with its contrasting textures and creamy colour, makes what is fundamentally a simple object seem like a precious artefact.

designed by
Akio Okumura, Japan
designer
Katsuji Minami
art director
Akio Okumura
client
Packaging Create Inc
printer
Packaging Create Inc
stock
hand-made

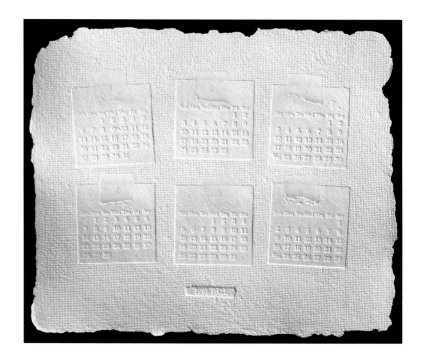

8

Sun	Mon	Tue	Wed	Thu	Fri	Sat
				1	2	3
	5	6	7	8	9	10
	13	14	15	16	17	
	20	21	22	23	24	
	27	28	29	30	31	

9

Sun	Mon	Tue	Wed	Thu	Fri	Sat
1	2	3	4	5	6	7
8	9	10	11	12	13	14
15	16	17	18	19	20	21
22	23	24	25	26	27	28
29	30					

11

Sun	Mon	Tue	Wed	Thu	Fri	Sat
					1	2

12

Sun	Mon	Tue	Wed	Thu	Fri	Sat
1	2	3	4	5	6	7

46 The natural colour and texture of the thick, pulpy card used to create this portfolio have been left unadorned, making them a key feature of the design. Blind debossing printing provides subtle, minimal graphics.

designed by
Akio Okumura, Japan
designer
Shuichi Nogami
art director
Akio Okumura
client
Packaging Create Inc
printer
Asahi Seihan Printing

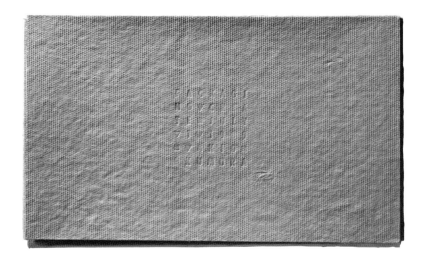

The thick card of this concertina-folded booklet has been deeply embossed and foil blocked to indicate both the shape and surface texture of a shell. The concertina-folded infill,which opens out to three times the size, is printed by an interesting technique using vaseline and alcohol.

designer
Irma Boom, Holland
printer
Drukkerij Rosbeek

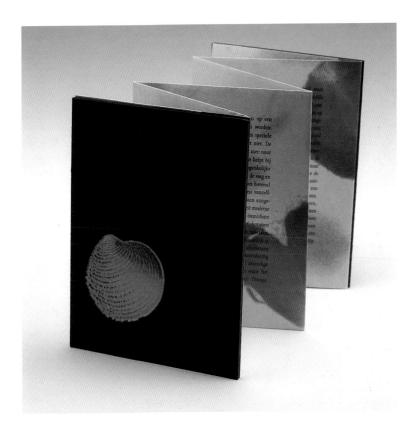

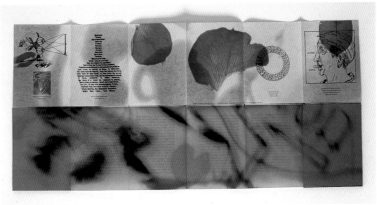

48 This New Year's card for 1980 exploits the reflective properties of metal foil: when the card is opened the circle and semi-circle double to form the number 80. At 90mm x 90mm, it is an unusually large area to be foil blocked, and the circle and semi-circle have themselves been blocked on top of the silver surface.

designed by
BK Wiese, Hamburg
designer
BK Wiese
client
Bruno and Ruth Wiese
printer
Bahruth, Reinbek

Caslon, Baskerville and Gill Sans, three quintessentially English typefaces, were the subject of this college project. Printed letterpress, it is an exploration of the aesthetics of each font and the letterpress process itself. Each section is printed on a different stock, chosen by the designer as being the most suitable for that face. Gill Sans, for instance, is on a crisp white satin stock, which complements its clean, functional design, whereas the older, serifed faces are on cream coloured papers with more textured, characterful surfaces.

designed by
Barbro Ohlson, London
client
Barbro Ohlson
stock
**Rivoli Natural 240gsm;
Arches Velin 270gsm;
Somerset White Satin
250gsm; Super Exelda
400gsm.**

50 The use of thick, deckle-edged paper, letterpress printing, and etched illustrations protected by sheets of glassine have given this book about the environment the appearence of a precious artifact. The intensely-coloured images bite into the surface of the paper, giving them a rich multi-layered texture which contrasts with the smoothness of the paper. Created as part of a college project, it was a collaboration between a designer and an illustrator.

designed by
Barbro Ohlson, London
illustrations by
Shonagh Rae
stock
**Somerset White Satin
250gsm**

Over-production of cattle for h

alternat

52 A traditional use of letterpress combined with die-stamping onto a textured stock emphasizes the subtle indentation of the type. The brief for the booklet, given to visitors of the Tullich Lodge Hotel, was that the design should reflect the simple, traditional architecture of the building. A die-stamped copper motif, and the tartan ribbon used to bind the pages together, provide contrast with the neutral, matt surface of the paper.

designed by
Imagination Design and Communication, London
designer
Lucy Richards
art director
Adrian Caddy
client
Tullich Lodge
printer
Baddeley Brothers
stock
cover: GB Flannel 217gsm
pages: GB Flannel 220gsm

TULLICH LODGE

A Warm v

Hector Macdonald a

Over the last decade it has b

your house in the country

ones, of great historic an

to be inhabited and m

54 The design of this stationery range was inspired by the name of the client, a furniture-making company called Pearl Dot, and the fact that each article of furniture they make is inlaid with a trade-mark pearl circle. Taking this as their focus, the designers printed the stationery with solid colour on the reverse, leaving a small white circle which shows through to the front. Attention was drawn to this by means of four registration marks. The colours and tones in which the stationery was printed were chosen to be reminiscent of the dyeline (blueprint) paper on which Pearl Dot's designs are created.

designed by
Lewis Moberly, London
designer
Judy Veal
art director
Mary Lewis
client
Pearl Dot
printer
Hector Martin
stock
Kaskad Osprey 110gsm

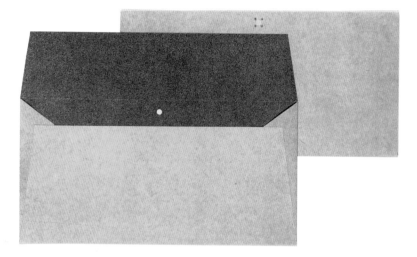

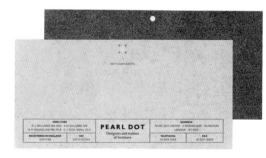

DIRECTORS
R J WILLIAMS MA MSc   A H WILLIAMS MA
S P HOUNSLOW MA RCA   C J ROSE MDes RCA

PEARL DOT
Designers and makers
of furniture

ADDRESS
PEARL DOT LIMITED   2 ROMAN WAY   ISLINGTON
LONDON   N7 8XG

REGISTERED IN ENGLAND	VAT		TELEPHONE	FAX
1294798	231 570 294		01 609 3169	01 607 3904

56 Transparent heat-sensitive thermochromic ink was used to cover the surface of this black christmas card. When handled or touched the seemingly blank card transforms 'before your very eyes'. The ink changes colour with the varying intensity of heat and can be specially made to take effect at pre-determined temperatures.

designed by
williams and phoa, London
designer
Sarah McKenzie
printer
B & H Group
stock
card: Keaykolour 300gsm
envelope: Keaykolour 135gsm

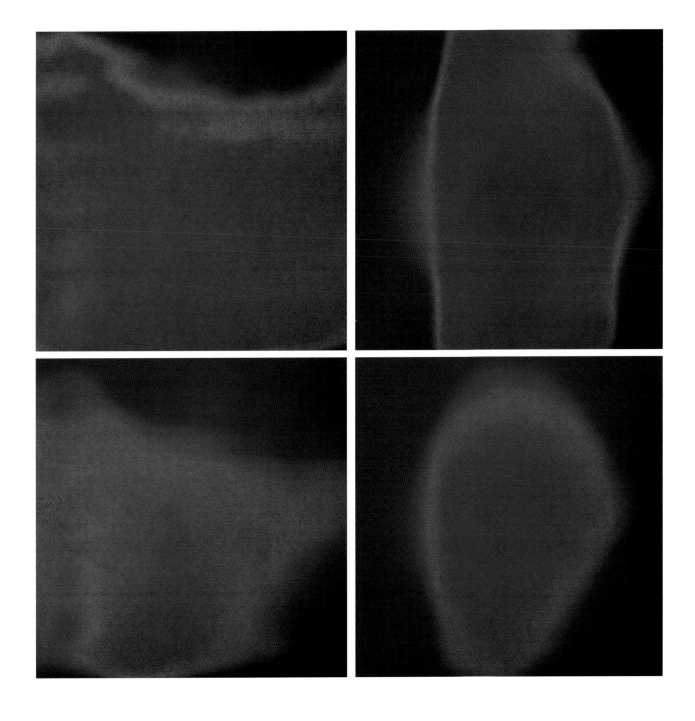

58 Opaque and transparent inks were silkscreened onto transparent drafting film to create a multi-layered image for this bold self-promotional poster. With two of the inks printed on to one side of the sheet, and four on the other, careful registration was essential, but the transparency of the stock was exploited to the full. Silkscreen was chosen for the strength and opacity of colour it allows.

designed by
Giant, London
designer
Neil Smith
art directors
Alan Herron, Martyn Hey, Neil Smith, Mark Rollinson
client
Giant
printer
Art-O-Matic
stock
drafting film

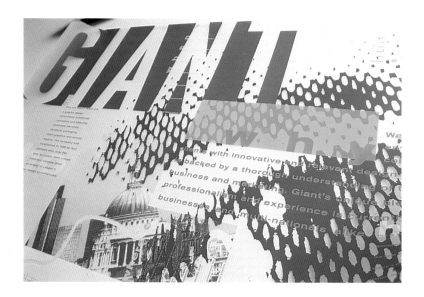

Rather than printing the client's logo directly on to their stationery, the designers decided to print it as a glossy, self-adhesive sticker which could be applied wherever needed. An unusual and fun form of tipping-in, both the colour and the glossy texture of the sticker provide a contrast with the paper on which the stationery is printed, and this approach allows the client, a small translation company, to 'customize' each letter.

designed by
Bull Rodger, London
designer
Laurence Grinter
art director
Paul Rodger
client
Talking Europe
stock
Croxley Script 100gsm,
JAC Brilliant Gloss
self-adhesive label paper

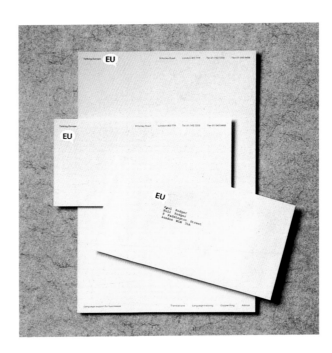

60   A mixture of traditional skills and
clean, modern design was used
to convey the range of possible
applications for the client's craft,
bookbinding. A small four-colour
tipped-in panel provides a
striking contrast of texture and
tone, facing a duotone
photograph printed full-bleed.
The thread-sewn, case-bound
book is a tangible example of
the client's work.

designed by
Silk Pearce, London
designers
**Jack Pearce, Harvey Lyon,
Andrew Ross**
art director
Jack Pearce
client
Hipwell Bookbinders
printer
Facsimile Printing Company
binder
Hipwell Bookbinders
stock
**Wiggins Teape Countryside,
Wiggins Teape Opal**

manipulation **paperwork**

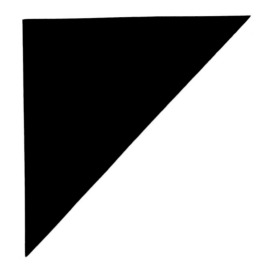

62 **techniques**

binding

cutting and folding

die-cutting

folding

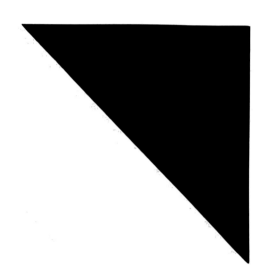

The techniques covered in this section are often overlooked; for example, cutting and folding are generally restricted to their most basic functions, such as windows, folder pockets and fold-outs while bindings are usually camouflaged rather than exploited.

Through the imaginative use of such simple techniques, however, a two-dimensional sheet of paper can be dramatically transformed. The effects achieved are often strongest when other printing techniques are kept to a minimum, allowing the manipulation of the paper to come to the fore.

Cutting and folding are not often considered as part of the designer's repertoire, but they can be used very effectively. For instance, just one edge of a brochure cut out of square can be used to add dynamism, as can a fold that is not perpendicular. The advantage of finishing techniques such as these is that they have to be done whether conventionally or not, and therefore 'playing' with them adds little or no cost to the job.

Die-cutting too can be an inexpensive and effective way of creating visual impact. There are three methods: in the cheaper version metal strips are bent to form the cutting edge, which imposes limits on the detail which can be achieved. For instance, right-angled corners will often not be perfect as the strips of metal may overlap or bend at the corner. True die-cutters, which are more expensive, allow for more intricate shapes as they are formed by acid-etching metal plates which carry a photographic image taken from artwork. For really intricate work, however, laser-cutting is the best technique as there is almost no limit to the detail possible or the materials that can be cut. Laser-cutting is, however, the most expensive method, although the cost may now drop as the number of finishers offering this service is increasing. It does, however, have a drawback: the laser beams leave a burnt edge, which is noticeable to varying degrees depending on the material which is being cut. As with any of these processes, it is worth finding the best finishers for the job.

Binding, the way that sheets of paper are fastened together or otherwise attached, can become the focal point of a design and it is in this area, almost more than any other, that designers are now using their ingenuity. Eyelets, inter-screws, string and elastic bands have all been used in various ways to bind together sheets of paper, often to great effect. Specially commissioned binding devices, such as those custom-made from metal, are becoming more common and are often used to give a smart, urbane look to brochures and catalogues. On the craft side, Japan has had its influence and on short runs Japanese techniques which leave the binding exposed give work a beautiful, hand-finished feel.

The following pages show a selection of examples where the designers have exploited both the paper's potential and the basic manipulative techniques in order to create work that is both imaginative and original.

A stunningly simple idea, the pages of this brochure are held together by a rubber band. This unusual binding allows the client, an art consultant, to update the pages easily when new artists are taken on. The client's high aesthetic standards and low budget have been met with a design which uses basic, inexpensive materials to create a brochure which is extremely sophisticated but does not overpower the images of the artists' work.

designed by
Chrissie Charlton & Company, London
designers
Chrissie Charlton, Chrissy Levett
client
Sarah Guinan Associates
printer
BFS

66 Although perfect bound, every
page of this exquisitely produced
book of poems and
photographs can be folded out
to double its size revealing a
previously hidden image.

designer
Irma Boom, Holland
printer
Drukkerij Rosbeek
stock
coffee-percolator paper

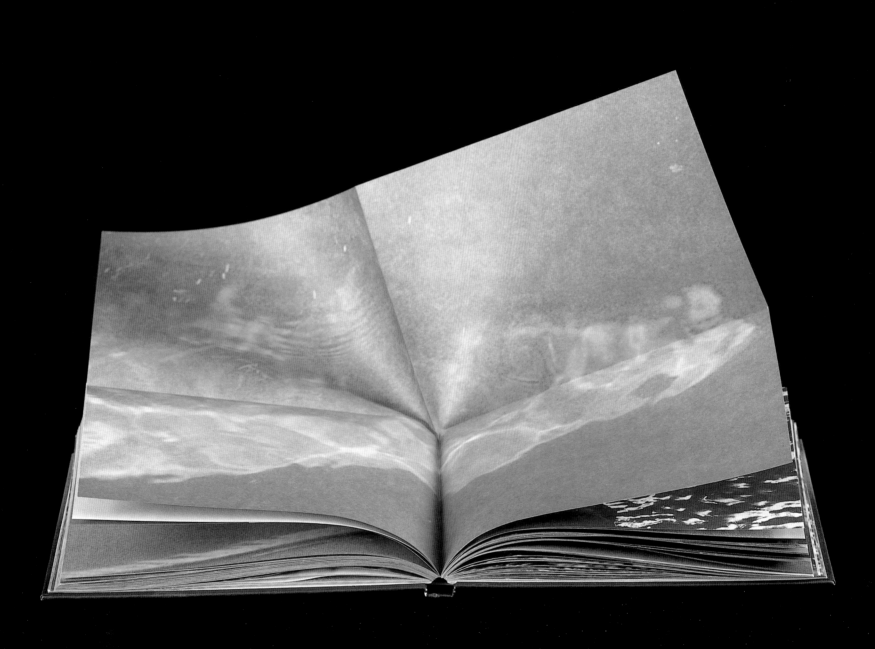

68 The two parts of an extruded aluminium binder slot together to hold the pages of this property brochure firmly in place. Designed so that new pages can be inserted, and different combinations sent to different clients, the binder has been screen-printed with the name of the development.

designed by
The Partners, London
designer
Peter Carrow
art director
David Stuart
client
Butlers Wharf
printer
Litho-tech

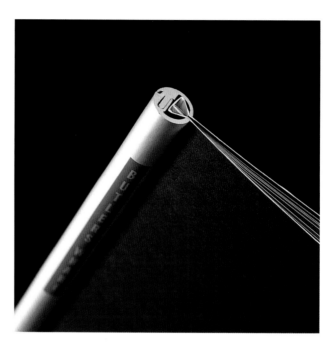

The binding of this brochure for an architectural practice was designed to take a number of inserts which were collated and bound by staff, as required. A simple but effective combination of folds, staples and double sided tape were used to achieve this.

designed by
williams and phoa, London
designers
Nancy Williams, Albert Kueh
client
Roughton and Fenton
printer
CTD
stock
cover: Elephant-hide 260gsm
text: Parilux Matt 170gsm

This British-designed booklet
uses traditional Japanese
binding techniques to reflect
the nature of its content: step-
by-step instructions on how
to make an origami flower.

designed by
The Partners, London
designers
Wendy Poulton, Aziz Cami
David Stuart, Nick Wurr
Malcolm Swatridge
art director
Malcolm Swatridge
stock
Whatman Watercolour

70 The concertina construction and free-standing nature of this promotional piece was used to reflect the fact that the client was a major organiser of exhibitions. As with most concertinas, this was printed in two sections which were glued together.

designed by
williams and phoa, London
designers
Phoa Kia Boon, Sarah McKenzie, Robert Mytton, Tim Webb-Jenkins
client
Blenheim Group plc
printer
CTD
stock
covers: Rodacote
text: Consort Royal Supreme Matt 250gsm

The triangular and heart-shaped
cardboard pages of this
brochure for a fashion designer
are presented in a flock-covered
slipcase, creating an odd
juxtaposition of colour, texture
and shape which was intended
to convey something of the
mood of the designer's latest
collection.

designed by
Area, London
designers
Richard Smith, Cara Gallardo
art director
Yvonne Sporre
client
Koji Tatsuno
printers
silkscreen: Art-O-Matic
packaging: Albany Packaging

72 Asked to create an invitation to
John Galliano's show which
would somehow reflect his new
collection, the designers created
an unusual, sculpturally shaped,
die-cut card. The combination of
its irregular shape, angled folds
and contrasting colours gives it
an intriguing appearance when
folded up to go in an envelope,
and would make it an interesting
object on any mantelpiece.
Despite its visual appeal it is a
simple design which would be
relatively inexpensive to produce.

designed by
Area, London
designers
Richard Smith, Cara Gallardo
art director
John Galliano
client
John Galliano
printer
Dot For Dot

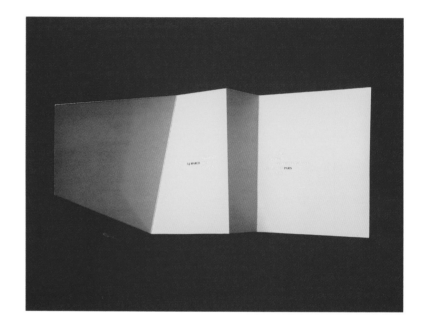

In this distinctive stationery for a food stylist, a dish of fresh strawberries - one of the stylist's raw materials - is turned into a dish of carefully arranged and styled fruits. On the compliments slip, the effect is achieved by flipping over the top of the paper; on the letterheading it happens when the letter is unfolded. Both only require a small amount of die-cutting and folding to create what is a very memorable visual identity.

designed by
Lewis Moberly, London
designer
Karin Dunbar
art director
Mary Lewis
client
Puff Fairclough
printer
Chater Press

SEE ME EAT ME

74 A mixture of die-cutting, folding and sewing has been used to create this poster. The designers have abandoned the clichéd rectangular outline in favour of a more complex solution suggestive of the items on display at the exhibition which the poster is advertising.

designed by
Igarashi Studio, Tokyo
designer
Takenobu Igarashi
client
Takenobu Igarashi
printer
Nissha Printing Company

In this greetings card, the
simplest of elements have
been combined to create a
satisfyingly complex design.
The mixture of die-cut letters
spelling the client's name,
overlapping process colours,
and a few folds, results in a card
which is an unusual mixture of
colour and shape.

designed by
**Fred Troller Associates,
New York**
client
Olympia U.S.A.

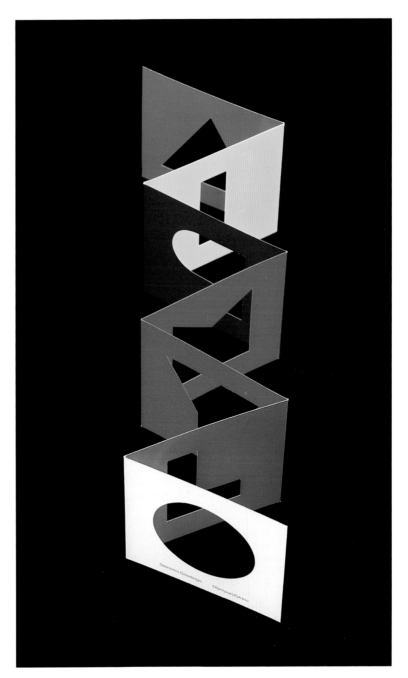

A delicate die-cut pattern, designed to represent a flower, makes an unusual illustration in this desk diary, a promotion for an offset printer. Because the image is die-cut the contrast between the colours is particularly sharp, and the purity of colour obtained from the single-colour litho printing is more like that of screen-printing.

designed by
George Tscherny Incorporated, New York
designers
Elisabeth Laub, Michelle Novak, Carla Tscherny, George Tscherny
art director
George Tscherny
client
Sandy Alexander Inc
printer
Sandy Alexander Inc

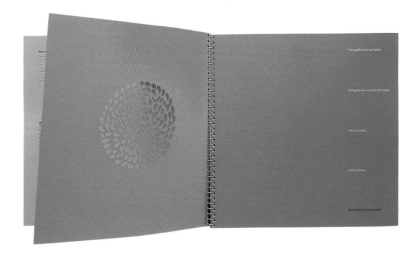

78 For this book containing the lyrics of twenty songs by the band New Order, the designers were inspired by the Roman numeral XX. While one of the Xs has been die-cut into the front cover, the second is revealed when the cover is opened. However, when the book was on sale it was wrapped in clear plastic on which an X-shaped sticker had been fixed, so that the XX was complete.

designed by
Pentagram, London
designers
Peter Saville, Brett Wickens, Marc Wood
client
Warner-Chappell Music

In this simple, powerful record
sleeve design, die-cut holes
in the blue outer sleeve reveal
the contrasting orange inner
sleeve inside. The design, done
in 1980, was inspired
by perforated steel used in
industrial architecture.

designed by
Ben Kelly, London
art director
Peter Saville
client
DinDisc

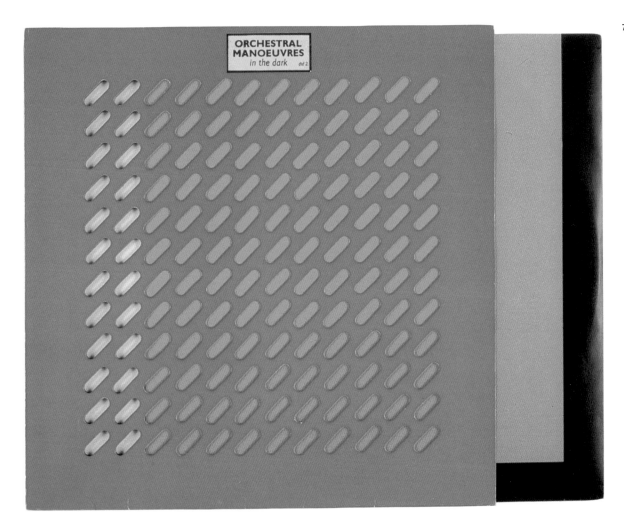

80 This promotional booklet for
a paper company uses
die- cutting to great effect. Each
spread promotes a different
property of the board, in this
instance moisture resistance.
The main element of each
illustration is a free-form die-cut
shape, which when pulled
back reveals a surprise.

designed by
The Partners, London
designers
Marita Lashko
Greg Quinton
art director
Aziz Cami
client
ISTD Papers
printer
Purley Press
stock
Pressboard 600gsm

This calendar for a typesetting company called Face uses die-cutting to witty effect. The eyes, nose and mouth have been die-cut to reveal the date details. This information is printed onto disks which project from the sides, creating the ears. The disks are held in place with eyelets which allow them to be turned to change the dates.

designed by
Pentagram, London
designer
John McConnell

82   In this first day cover book,
created to promote newly issued
stamps, die-cutting has been
used to mimic stamp
perforations so that the
illustrations of the new issues
seem as much like real stamps
as possible. For a section about
stamps celebrating the work of
the crime writer Agatha Christie,
die-cut perforations were again
used, this time to imitate the
chalk lines which, in detective
stories, the police draw around
bodies.

designed by
Trickett and Webb, London
designer
Andrew Thomas
client
Royal Mail
printer
The House of Questa Ltd

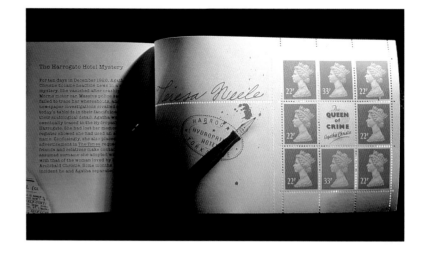

S BREAD

atha Christie, Na...
nishing *Giant'...*
 then unkno...
ead a book...
w let me...
at's it – ...
ildren...
rectly.

e ar...
com...
the...
mor...
of th...
e hi...
de...
o...
...

New generations have come to
appreciate the whodunit skills of
Agatha Christie since her death in 1976.
Television adaptations of the Miss Marple and
Poirot books have achieved critical acclaim as
well as popular success. The crime novels
themselves remain best sellers. On stage,
The Mousetrap *runs and runs
and runs.*

84   A play on the name of the client
company, POD, this calender
uses die-cutting to create three-
dimensional models of pea pods
filled with peas. Careful
alignment of the die-cutting and
the printing on both sides of the
sheet was necessary to make
the idea work.

designed by
Pentagram, New York
designer
Woody Pirtle
client
POD
printer
Williamson

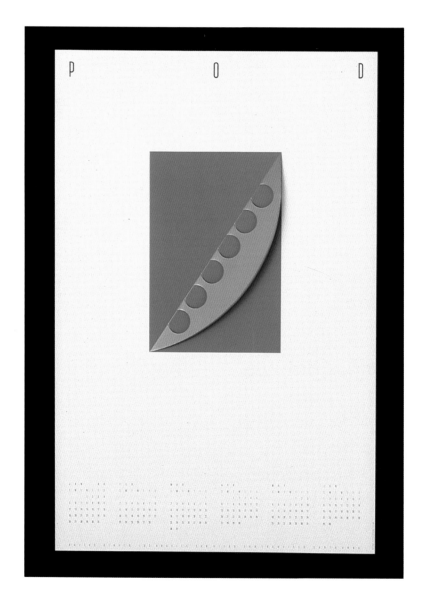

Here, die-cutting has been used as a practical and aesthetically appealing solution to a packaging problem. The shape of the woman's leg has been cut out of the package so that the colour and texture of the product within can be clearly seen. However, unlike many other hosiery packs, the die-cut window forms an integral part of the graphic design.

designed by
Lewis Moberly, London
designers
David Booth, Mary Lewis,
Lucilla Scrimgeour
art director
Mary Lewis
client
The Boots Company

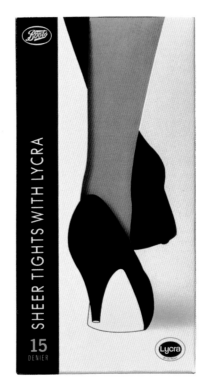

86 The die-cut holes in this card were strategically positioned so that the lettering inside could not be seen and the card appeared blank. When opened, the hidden message is revealed.

designed by
**M Plus M Incorporated,
New York**
designer
Takaaki Matsumoto
client
Knoll International
printer
CGS

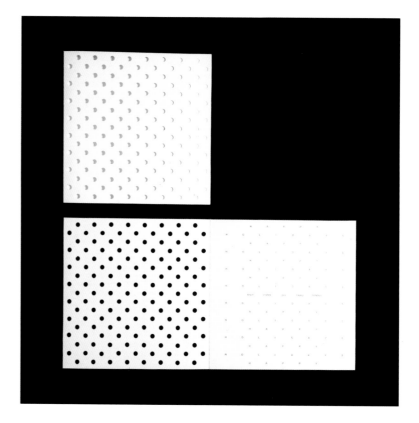

Half die-cut feminine curves and copper plate, half resolute straight edges and sans serif, this personal stationery was designed for a couple, each of whom can use it a different way up. If both are writing, the paper can be folded so that their names appear together.

designed by
williams and phoa, London
clients
Bukola French, Ivor French
stock
**Mellotex Matt Super White
115 gsm**

88 Recipients of this calendar, a
promotion for the Face
Photosetting company, were
expected to participate in its
creation by folding out the die-
cut sections, and the holes left
by the fold-outs become part of
the images, as well as the
folded-out sections themselves.
A mixture of shadows and
colours printed on the back of
the card were used to create
the faces.

designed by
Pentagram, London
designer
John McConnell
client
Face Photosetting

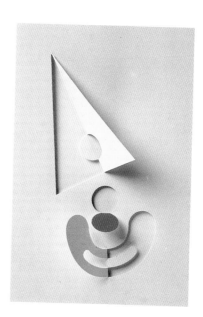

90 Designed for a caterer, this
stationery has die-cut 'bites'
taken out of it, a simple but
humorous allusion to her work.
Die-cutting was used in an
equally humorous manner for the
client's moving card, in which
slots were cut to hold an
updated business card in such a
way that it looked like a removal
van. The inserted card, printed
with the company's new
address, could be removed and
kept for reference.

designed by
Pentagram, London
designers
John Rushworth, Vince Frost
client
Celia Keyworth

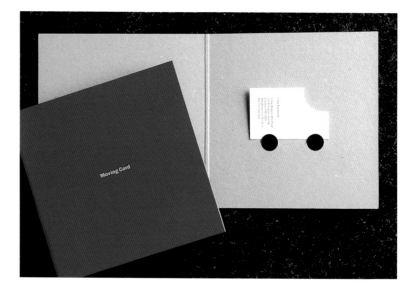

The expensive, but extremely accurate, process of laser-cutting has been used here to create a pattern which is so delicate it almost resembles a swatch of fabric.

designed by
Igarashi Studio, Tokyo
designer
Yukimi Sasago
art director
Takenobu Igarashi
client
Axis

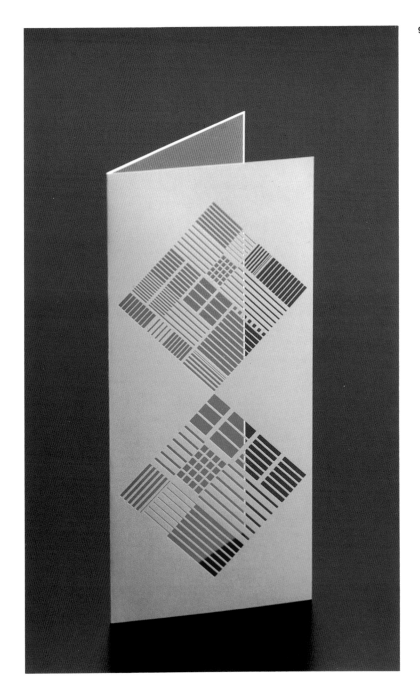

92 This stationery for a masseuse is a simple visual pun on her occupation. The typography, set in the shape of a hand, seems to be massaging the crumpled paper to smooth it. Each sheet of the paper, which was chosen to convey something of the texture and colour of skin, has to be crumpled by hand before being used.

designed by
Bull Rodger, London
designer
John Bull
art director
Paul Rodger
client
Nina Triggs
stock
**GF Smith Colour plan
100gsm**

At first glance this diary, produced in conjunction with a typesetter, a lithographer and a printer, appears to be purely typographic. Illustrations are, however, hidden behind fold-outs to excite the reader's curiosity.

designer
Una, Holland
client
self-promotion

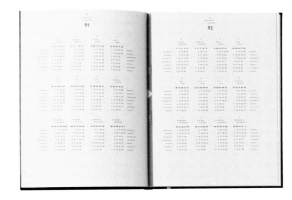

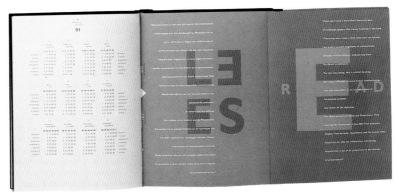

94   In this information pack for the
Student Awards run by the UK's
Design and Art Direction
organization, the file which
contains the information sheets
can be unfolded into a poster.
The image on the poster can be
seen in two ways: either as a
megaphone shouting out the
information, or as the lead in a
yellow pencil, the Design and Art
Direction Association's symbol.

designed by
Lewis Moberly, London
designers
**Karin Dunbar,
Bruce Duckworth**
art director
Mary Lewis
client
Design and Art Direction
printer
Chater Press

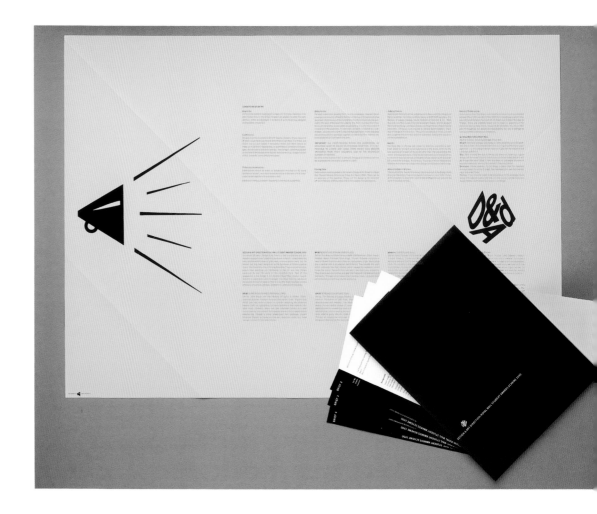

three dimensions **paperwork**

96 **techniques**

packaging

pop-up

products

sculpture

Paper and card offer enormous potential for three-dimensional design. Unfortunately this is rarely exploited in the West, perhaps for reasons of cost - often this work requires laborious hand finishing. In Japan, however, ingeniously intricate structures and containers are common. Sometimes they are created from single sheets of paper or card folded in such a way that there is no need for staples or glue, a mixture of simplicity and complexity which gives them a unique charm.

The advantage of using folded paper or card structures for packaging is that they can be very strong; when folded in certain ways a single flimsy sheet can take on a remarkable rigidity, ideal for packaging. Nevertheless, cardboard engineering, as it is known, is rarely used in this area, other than in its most basic form, probably for commercial reasons.

Designs which require a lot of work by hand may have to be sent long distances to places where labour is cheaper. However, such packaging can be a very efficient use of materials, which may make it more popular as the rebellion against over-packaging grows.

Pop-ups, on the other hand, are becoming more popular especially in greetings cards and books. The element of surprise when a two-dimensional object is transformed into three dimensions generates and maintains interest because of the viewer's interaction with it. Because of the labour-intensive finishing which can be required, the cardboard engineers who create these objects have to use their skills to get the maximum effect from the smallest number of pieces, avoiding glueing wherever possible, if the design is going to be economical to produce.

As a material for sculpture, paper is not as popular a medium as it was in the 1970s, and there are few people now who have the necessary skill. Often too flamboyant, much of the paper sculpture done today tends to verge on the kitsch. There is, of course, no reason why it should; perhaps it is time to look at it again.

Because of its tremendous versatility, paper has also been used for a very wide variety of products: loudspeaker cones, lampshades, disposable clothing and even wedding dresses. Lloyd Loom, the wicker-like furniture which became popular in the early part of the century, is made of varnished twisted paper and many early examples are still in use - a testimony to its durability.

We should not, then, assume that paper is disposable material only suitable for ephemera: approached with an open mind, in the hands of an imaginative designer, paper can be used to create almost anything.

The examples in this section have been restricted to those produced by graphic designers. They do, however, demonstrate the way that paper successfully lends itself to the third dimension.

98 The thick, rough texture of this
packaging provides an
interesting contrast with the
smooth, shiny glassware it
protects.

designer
Akio Okumura, Japan
client
Kazu Jewelry Design Studio
printer
Packaging Create

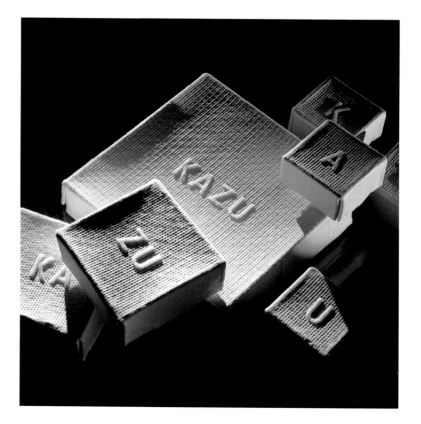

The robust, utilitarian box in
which this range of towels is
packaged can be transformed
into a display case by means of
its string fastening.

designed by
Akio Okumura, Japan
designer
Mikito Tanaka
art director
Akio Okumura
client
Uchino
printer
Taihei Printing

100 A mixture of thick, flexible paper
and stainless-steel panels was
used to create a visually exciting
and suitably robust container for
earthenware products. The
dramatic contrast between the
soft, crinkly, matt texture of the
paper and the smooth, hard,
shiny steel makes this a
particularly tactile and intriguing
design.

designed by
Akio Okumura, Japan
designer
Akio Okumura
client
Seibu
printer
Packaging Create

This range of unusually shaped
boxes was designed to take tap
fittings with the minimum of
wasted space. Each box was
constructed from only two
pieces of card, held together by
a series of ingenious folds, tabs
and slots.

designed by
Pentagram, London
art director
David Hillman
designer
Nancy Williams
client
Ideal Standard
stock
'B' flute corrugated

102   Textured recycled paper, metal hinges, unusual fastenings and blind embossed hallmarks were combined to produce packaging which would appeal to the aesthetic sensibilities of the designers and illustrators who would be using this range of pencils. The result is lavish but subtle.

designed by
Newell and Sorrell, London
designer
Derick Hudspith
art directors
Frances Newell, John Sorrell
client
Berol

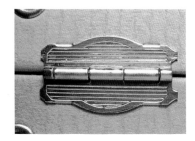

104 Interest was added to this
moving card by the church
portico which pops up when the
card is opened. The designers,
who were their own clients on
this project, got their
ecclesiastical theme from the
architecture of their new studio,
which had formerly been a
church.

designed by
Keeble & Hall, London
designer
Imogen Davis
art director
Janine Hall, Chris Keeble
client
Keeble & Hall
printer
Taylor Bloxham
stock
**Ikonorex Special Matt
Ivory 250gsm**

What might otherwise have been a dull biology book was made fun by the inclusion of a number of pop-up and movable illustrations, which very graphically illustrate the workings of the human body.

designed by
Pentagram, London
designer
David Pelham
client
Jonathan Cape

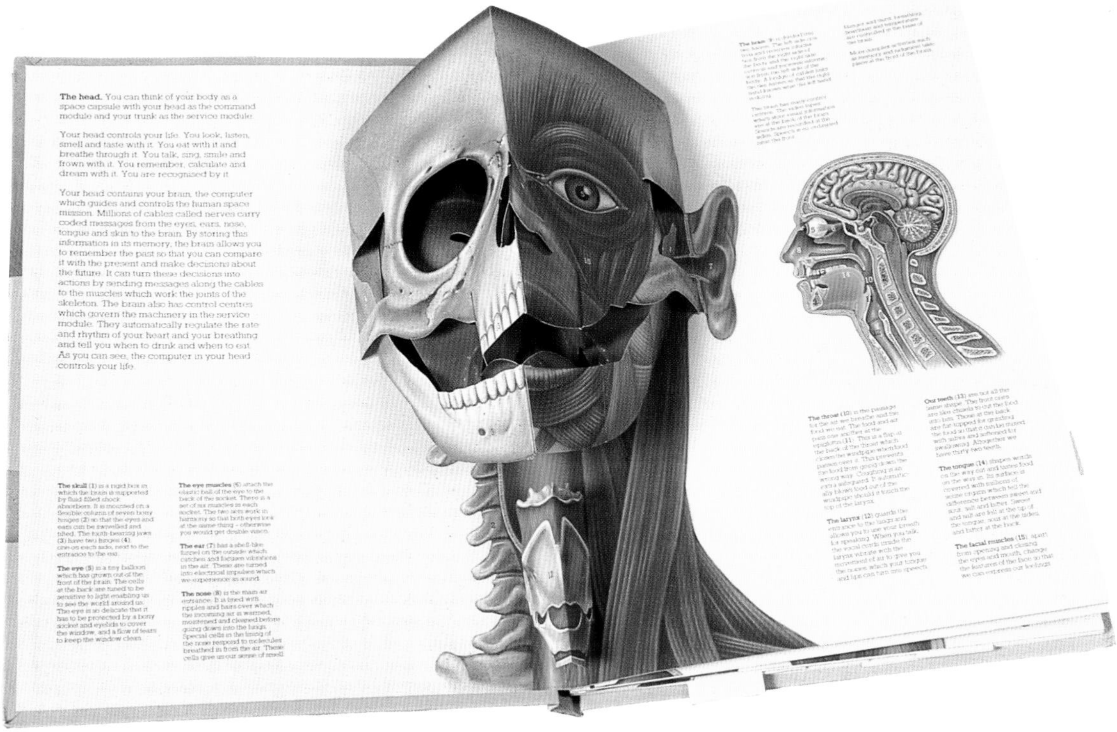

106 The designers of this range of
stationery folders took a new
look at an old material, papier
mâché, usually thought only
suitable for cheap, disposable
packaging. By dying the
newspaper pulp and mixing it
with beeswax, they created a
material which was evenly
coloured and waterproof,
resulting in a range with a
chunky, grainy aesthetic unusual
for such products.

designed by
**Priestman Associates,
London**
designer
Nigel Goode
art directors
Nigel Goode, Paul Priestman
client
Colourstyle
printer
Colourstyle

108 Various paper qualities have been exploited in the production of these clocks. Both versions are based on simple two-part constructions, rivetted together. Holes are die-cut into the front surface to take the hands and in the back to access the movement. For one clock, the smooth surface of a coated card was silkscreened with metallic and fluorescent inks; light falling on its curved face is absorbed, reflected and dissipated. The calligraphic pattern on the surface of the other clock was embossed into heavily textured watercolour paper to create a smoothly ridged effect, and at 530mm x 370mm was the largest area it was possible to have embossed. The clocks were presented in a one piece corrugated carrying case.

designed by
williams and phoa, London
designers
Phoa Kia Boon
Richard Bonner Morgan
client
williams and phoa
printer
silkscreen: Art-O-Matic
embossing: Foil Ribbon and
Impact Printing
finisher
clocks: RHB Print Finishers
cases: Duffin Containers
stock
Keaykolour Bockingford Not
Coated carton board
Mounting board
Craft B flute

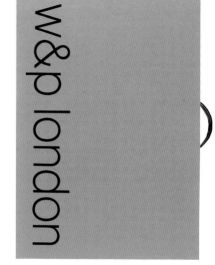

w & p london

110   These clocks were developed to answer specific briefs posed by a variety of clients: a promotional piece for Finsbury Dials, a modern development in the City of London; a gift to mark a new identity for an architectural client and a clock to emphasise the importance of Leeds as a financial centre. Once again a variety of techniques were used in their production.

designed by
williams & phoa, London
designers
David Baird, Laura Heard
Phoa Kia Boon, Nancy
Williams
clients
Norwich Union Insurance
Group, TTSP, Scope
printers
letterpress: Hand and Eye
silk screen: Art-O-Matic
finisher
RHB Print Finishers
stock
Coated carton board
Bockingford Not
Mounting board

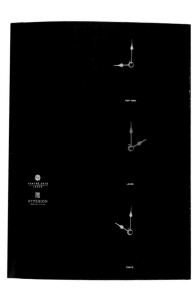

A satisfying combination of solid cast iron base, elegant spiral holder and delicate paper shade provide a pleasing balance of materials and textures in this side-light.

designed by
Igarashi Studio, Tokyo
designer
Takenobu Igarashi
client
Yamada Shomei Lighting
materials
cast iron, washi paper

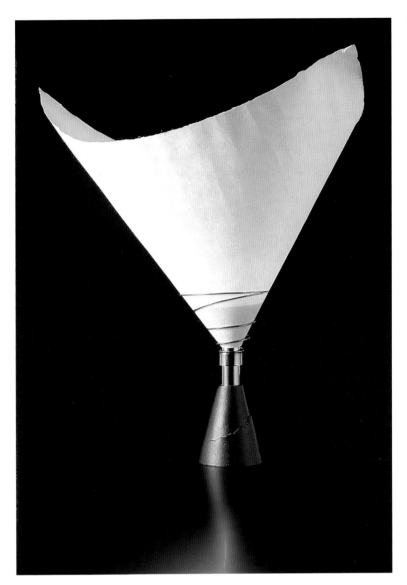

112 The three-dimensional effect of
the paper sculpture tower
inserted into this wine label for
La Tour Carnet brings an
otherwise low-key design to life.

designed by
Halpin Grey Vermeir, London
designer
Pierre Vermeir
client
Halpin Grey Vermeir
printer
M & M

Although paper is incredibly versatile it is exciting to ring the changes occasionally. Graphics can be applied to anything: cloth, plastics, metal and rubber, for instance, can all be incorporated into designs. Many designers are experimenting with the unexpected textures of out-of-the-ordinary materials to create objects which surprise and intrigue and so engage the viewer's interest.

Invitations, catalogues and corporate brochures made of plastic, metal or even glass are now to be seen with unexpected regularity, as well as designs for exhibitions, which, perhaps because they are semi-architectural, have long incorporated the use of such materials.

Plastic paper such as Tyvek, Polyart and Dyverse, seemingly the most obvious alternative to paper, is very seldom used. Apart from envelopes it is rarely seen, although there must be uses to which this strong, washable, virtually indestructible material can be put - it would, for instance, seem ideal for manuals and children's books.

Since the 1950s when plastics were championed as being the epitome of modernity there has been a backlash against them, but now graphic designers are using them very creatively, experimenting with their various textures and opacities and exploiting the purity of colour they offer. With the exception of the plastic papers, most plastics have had to be printed using either the silk screen or flexographic processes. However, it is now possible to print plastic sheets using offset litho, although the static build-up can create problems for the printer.

Metal is an alternative that is being used more and more and is available in thin enough weights to be used for brochure covers and business cards. Images can be applied by silkscreen or acid etching and lasers can be used to cut intricate patterns into or through the surface. In addition, surface effects such as verdigris can be created by chemically treating the surface.

The use of cloth has mainly been restricted to book binding and children's books, but there is no reason why it should not be used more extensively on small quantities. For example Vylene, the fabric used for stiffening collars and so on, is a stable synthetic material which can, with reasonable care, be printed. Its advantage over woven cloth is that the edges do not have to be finished off because its bonded fibres prevent fraying. Its durability, flexibility and washability are surely properties that could be exploited further.

With any of these materials the main problem is often finding a printer or finisher with experience of them, or one who is willing to experiment. The following examples show how worthwhile this experimental process can be.

116 Thin layers of gauzy cotton attached to backings of recycled paper make this poster, brochure and card tactile and eyecatching. Designed to promote an exhibition of work by a fabric designer, using a mixture of screen printing and litho, they are an example of very simple materials and techniques used to engage the viewer's interest.

designed by
Andrea Muheim, Bolzano
art director
Marco Philipp
printer
Reprof ag CH Gurtnellen
client
Muheim family

The corrugated cardboard which protects this design is usually used for packaging bottles. Here it wraps an aluminium folder containing limited-edition prints, a tenth anniversary present from a firm of architects to its clients. The two sheets of aluminium - a metal chosen because it is the traditional tenth anniversary material - are held together by two Philips screws, chosen because the cross on the head of one of them forms the ampersand in the company's name, engraved on either side.

designed by
williams and phoa, London
designers
Albert Kueh, Nancy Williams
client
Jestico & Whiles
printer
Litho-tech
metalwork
Respoire Architectural
stock
metal: aluminium sheeting
6 gauge
sleeve: expandable
corrugated board
prints: Consort Royal
Supreme Matt

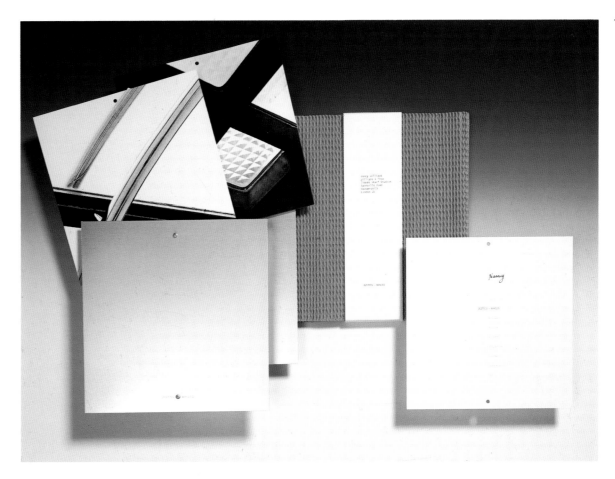

118   Asked to design a catalogue which could be easily updated, M Plus M took a different route from the usual solution of a ring-binder and hole-punched pages. Instead, the loose-leaf sheets were presented in a smart and tough anodized aluminium box, screen-printed with the client's name.

designed by
M Plus M Incorporated, New York
designer
Takaaki Matsumoto
client
Comme des Garcons
printers
Nissha Printing, Saunders Manufacturing

Squares of vividly coloured see-through perspex held in place by contrasting rubber bands form the cover of the brochure for fashion designer Koji Tatsuno. Removing the cover is like opening a present; inside, the unbound pages are on a mixture of stocks, ranging from dull sugar paper to high-gloss silk, printed with bright, atmospheric images. The combination of materials, textures, colours and surfaces makes this unusually exciting.

designed by
Area, London
designers
Richard Smith, Cara Gallardo
art director
Yvonne Sporre
client
Koji Tatsuno
printers
silkscreen: Art-O-Matic
litho: Dot For Dot
materials
perspex: Haymar Acrylic
rubber bands: Pentonville
Rubber

Filled with brightly coloured liquid, these floppy plastic invitations for fashion designer John Galliano's show are immensely tactile and difficult to ignore. The graphics were silk-screened on to the pvc bags, which had to be robust enough to survive sending through the mail without leaking.

designed by
Area, London
designers
Richard Smith, Cara Gallardo
art director
John Galliano
client
John Galliano
printers/suppliers
bags: **A& A Vacuum Packing**
invitations: **Art-O-Matic**
labels: **Richard Harden**
stock
bags: **clear rigid pvc**
120 micron
labels: **transtext self-**
adhesive

122 A simple but effective design of
bold silk-screened graphics on a
transparent plastic bag.

designed by
Signo, Milan
designer
Heinz Waibl
client
Bticino

The clear plastic cover of this brochure is filled with water and coins. It is an unusual use of materials, the result of a brief which asked for a memorable promotion for a property development called The Fountains. The idea was a play on the tradition of throwing coins into fountains for good luck.

designed by
The Partners, London
designer
Martin McLoughlin
art director
Steve Gibbons
printers
screen: Art-O-Matic
litho: Fulmar
client
Five Oaks Investments

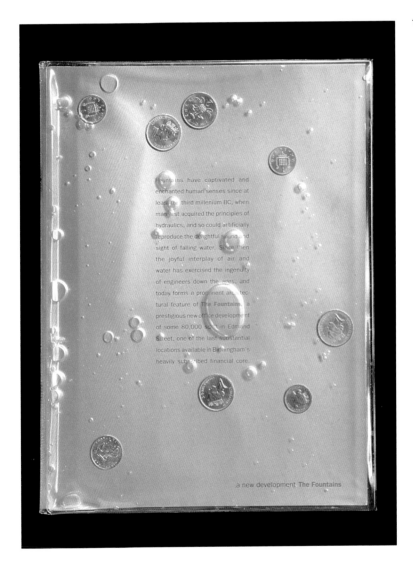

124 According to tradition, anniversaries are associated with special materials such as silver and gold. It is less well known that the material for a second anniversary is rag. Inspired by this, design company The Partners made a rag book to celebrate its second anniversary. A pastiche of the rag books sometimes given to small children, it is printed with brightly coloured images illustrating famous partnerships.

designed by
The Partners, London
designer
David Stuart
client
The Partners
printer
Planet Display
stock
100% cotton

TQ, a furniture company which specialized in one-off pieces, needed a brochure which would demonstrate its craft skills to its potential clients, interior designers. Given the small print run, the brochure's designers were able to experiment with materials and techniques which required hand finishing. The result is a booklet which, like the furniture it advertises, is mostly made of wood.

designed by
Giant, London
client
TQ
materials
Aircraft plywood, draw film

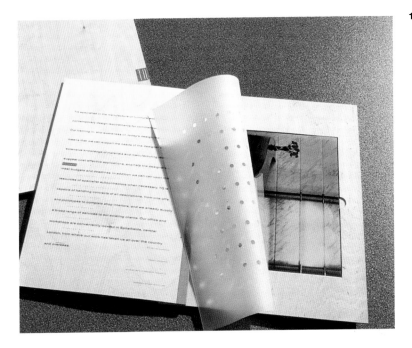

Slices of wood from storm-damaged trees were turned into invitations for an unusual Alpine-themed Christmas party held by a design company. The text was added by the designers themselves, using a blow-torch to heat up the specially made embossing tool so that the words were burnt into the surface of the wood.

designed by
Giant, London
client
Giant

126 These three bi-monthly calendars were hand-assembled by the designer from a range of materials including plywood, paper, steel rods and washers. A combination of the detail of the graphics, the sculptural curves of the plywood and the delicacy with which the paper has been cut and folded has given them the feel of precious artefacts despite the ordinariness of the materials from which they have been made.

designed by
Nick Bell, London
client
Peter Milne Furniture Makers
stock
Simulator 160gsm
Consort Royal Supreme Matt
135gsm
materials
birch-faced aeroply 1.5mm,
threaded steel rods, nuts,
washers

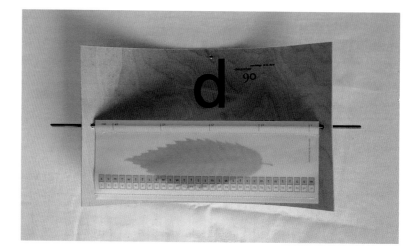

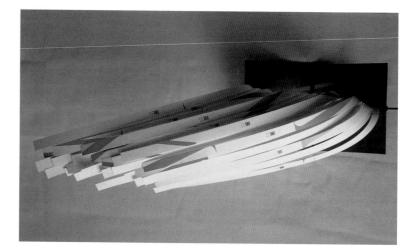

sun risings: 06.38–05.36

april

a 91

sun settings: 7.32–8.21

april

29 m	30 t					
pm	pm					
22 m	23 t	24 w	25 t	26 f	27 s	28 s
pm	pm	pm	pm	pm	pm	pm
15 m	16 t	17 w	18 t	19 f	20 s	21 s
pm	pm	pm	pm	pm	pm	pm
8 m	9 t	10 w	11 t	12 f	13 s	14 s
pm	pm	pm	pm	pm	pm	pm
1 m	2 t	3 w	4 t	5 f	6 s	7 s
pm	pm	pm	pm	pm	pm	pm

14

week

128 Made of ebony and cypress wood, this puzzle was created as a promotion for a furniture company. The precision of the cutting and finishing and the texture and colours of the wood act as visual and tactile reminders of the company's products.

designed by
Signo, Milan
designer
Heinz Waibl
client
Linea Legno

mixed media **paperwork**

130 **techniques**

mixed

As most of the individual techniques and effects which graphic designers can use have been covered in the previous sections, there is little to add here. However, as the images in this section illustrate, the judicious combination of such techniques and media can lead to exciting contrasts of texture, colour and tactile qualities which can startle, intrigue or delight the viewer.

Interestingly, it appears that the designers who are most imaginative in their use of different papers tend also to be those who are most open to the possibilities of creating work which uses a rich mixture of materials and effects. Consequently, many of the designers whose work has been included in this section are those whose work can also be found scattered throughout the book.

132   By reconsidering a very ordinary
material, bubble wrap, the
designer of this calendar has
created an object which is
simple, functional and great fun.

designed by
Akio Okumura, Japan
designer
Takeshi Kusumoto
art director
Akio Okumura
client
Packaging Create
printer
Inoue Paper

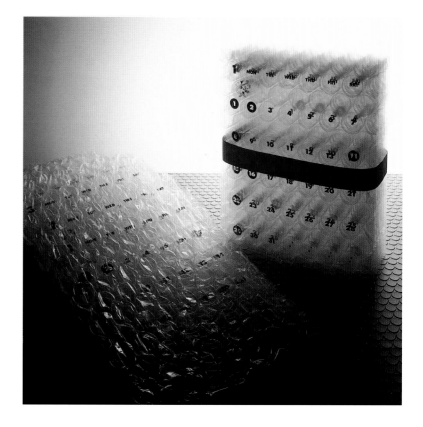

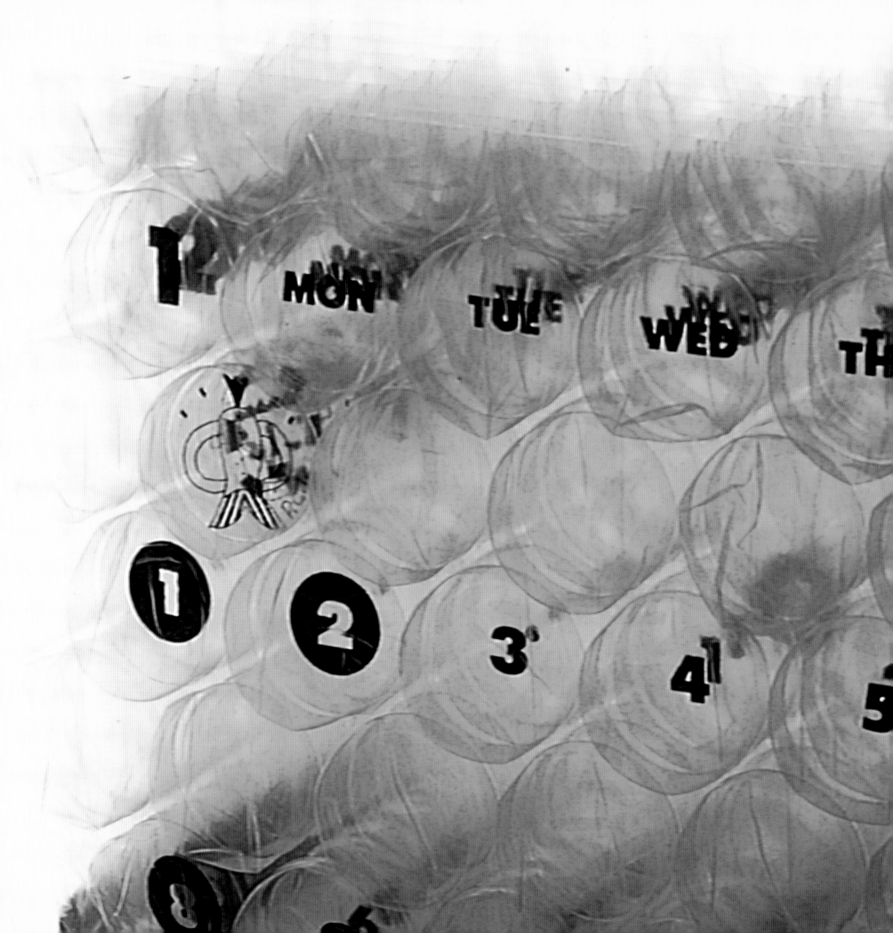

134 Wrapped in protective
corrugated cardboard, tied with
string and sealing-wax, the
packaging for this self-
promotional booklet on the
theme of music shows how very
basic materials can be used to
add fun to a project.

designed by
Benoit Jacques, Paris
client
Benoit Jacques
materials
**corrugated card, string,
sealing-wax**

mixed **paperwork**

A self-promotional piece which combines a wide range of stocks and effects, including blind embossing, tipping-in, foil blocking and individual numbering. On opening the booklet, the viewer is surprised by its torn pages, which appear to be corners from letterheads and are there as examples of the designers' work. To incorporate these into the booklet, the pages had to be hand-torn and then sewn in.

designed by
Bull Rodger, London
designer
Laurence Grinter
art director
John Bull
client
Bull Rodger
stock
text: uncoated cartridge
135gsm
cover: coated cartridge
200gsm

136 Hand-applied metal
reinforcements reminiscent of
those found on furniture give this
calendar a traditional craft feel at
odds with the modernity of the
minimalist graphics. The
calendar, packaged in a tube,
was made of Fabriano paper.
This stock was chosen because
of its ability to absorb moisture
from the atmosphere, so
that once unrolled it would
quickly flatten out.

designed by
clean, London
designer
Stephen A Taylor
stock
**Fabriano Rosaspina bianco
220gsm**

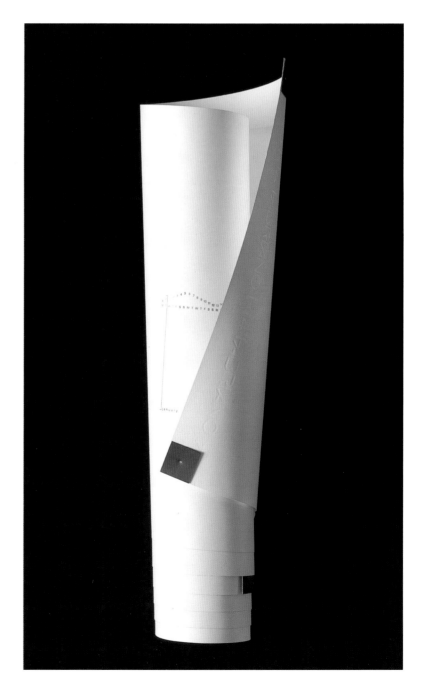

Bubble wrap and corrugated cardboard - typical packaging materials - were used to 'package' this brochure for the British Rail Parcels Group. Designed both to raise awareness of the Group within British Rail as a whole, and to encourage new corporate business, the brochure is an example of very ordinary materials being used in a witty and attractive way.

designed by
Roundel Design Group, London
designers
Michael Denny, John Bateson, Darren Richardson, Sarah Perry
client
British Rail Parcels Group
materials
single-sided flute board, bubble-wrap, Consort Royal Supreme Silk 200gsm

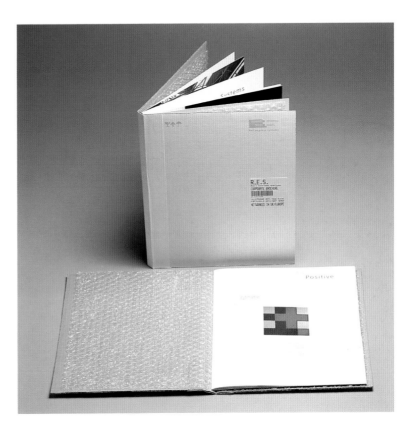

138 In this stationery range a number of different techniques, including blind embossing, die-cutting and foil blocking, have been used to achieve a rich visual texture. Many items have been designed using techniques which affect both sides of the paper; the business card, for instance, has been punched with a hole which links the company name on the front to the designer's name on the reverse.

designed by
Koeweiden Postma, Holland
client
Koeweiden Postma

140 Based on a line from W.B. Yeats'
poem *Cuchulain Myths*, and
influenced by the work of
Joseph Beuys, 'six mortal
wounds' is an elaborate self-
promotional mailer in which the
process of unwrapping the
packaging - which includes loft
insulation foam, drafting film and
cardboard - is as important as
discovering the contents. The
insulation protects a transparent
envelope, fastened with waxed
bookbinders' string and a fishing
weight. The envelope contains
smaller envelopes which
themselves contain cards
representing the 'wounds to
humanity'.

designed by
Nick Bell, London
designer
Nick Bell
client
Nick Bell
materials
**envelope: Italian Ingres
Fabriano 80gsm
translucent wallet: Uno
drafting film
holding block: loft insulation
foam
block surround: corrugated
cardboard
wallet enclosure: lead fishing
weight, waxed bookbinders'
string**

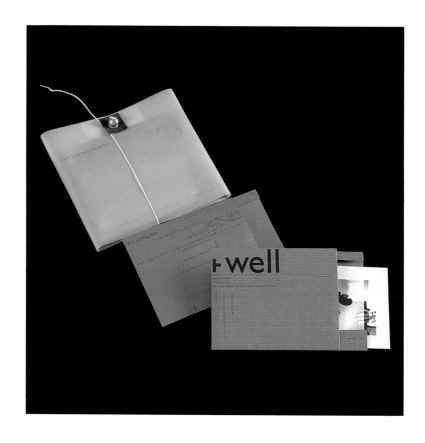

The front cover of this book is a piece of polished wood, the back cover a wood-patterned laminate; the two sides were attached with a traditional cloth quarter binding. The text pages carry tipped-in images relating to the copy. Created as a self-promotion, it celebrates the fifth anniversary of a design company, and is one of a series of such booklets. Each year's book has been based on the material which is traditionally associated with that year's anniversary.

designed by
The Partners, London
designer
Shaun Dew
client
The Partners
printers
CTD, Anderson Fraser

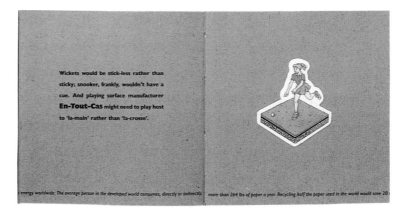

Wickets would be stick-less rather than sticky; snooker, frankly, wouldn't have a cue. And playing surface manufacturer **En-Tout-Cas** might need to play host to 'la-main' rather than 'la-crosse'.

142 The cover of this brochure for
two glass artists is a physical
reminder of the material they
work with. The glass of which it
is made has been etched with
the 'fragile' pictogram, and wire-
bound to the rest of the
brochure's pages.

designed by
Pentagram, London
designers
**John Rushworth, Lorenzo
Shakespear**
client
Radford & Ball

FRAGILE

144 The clear, colourless plastic
wrap-around covers on this set
of brochures for an architect
were printed using a mixture of
litho and silkscreen on the
reverse, with the name of each
building reversed out of the
photographic image so that the
white paper beneath shows
through. Inside the booklets,
technical drawings, computer-
generated images and almost
abstract photographs of details
of the architect's scale models
give an unusually impressionistic
view of his buildings. The text
pages were singer sewn along
the spine - an exacting task for
the finisher.

designed by
williams and phoa, London
designers
Phoa Kia Boon
Sarah McKenzie
client
Peter Foggo
printer
CTD
stock
cover: Huntsman mark
resistant 140 microns
text: Parilux matt white
200 gsm

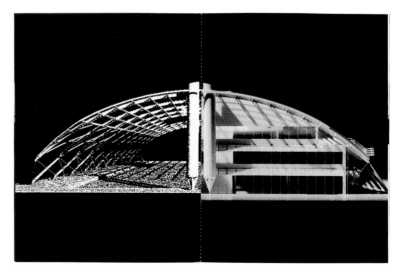

W2 Stockley Park

Peter Foggo Associates

15 Chiswick Park Square

Peter Foggo Associates

40 Queen Victoria Street

146 This range of stationery for a lighting consultancy relies on light for its effect. The back of the letterheading has been printed solid black - except for the company's name which has been reversed out in mirror writing. When the paper is held to the light the name is illuminated and appears the right way round. The business 'cards' are in fact black-printed plastic, with the company name left see-through, and the other details printed on the black surface in black ink so that they only show up when light hits the card from a certain angle.

designed by
williams and phoa, London
designer
Laura Heard
client
Konu & Morrow
printers
Art-O-Matic
stock
**letterhead: Mellotex Ultra White 115 gsm
business card: Huntsman mark resistant 220 microns**

An invitation to celebrate five years in business. The outer card was debossed to house a musical mechanism which played the tune 'happy birthday' when opened. The device was triggered by a die-cut slot in the blue insert which was tipped-in to the outer card.

designed by
williams and phoa, London
designers
Nancy Williams
Phoa Kia Boon
client
williams and phoa
printers
Face
stock
Fabriano Designo

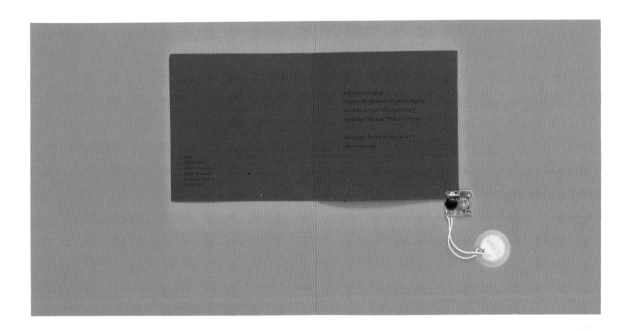

148 In response to a brief from D&AD and Royal Mail to reduce the cost and increase the efficiency of a briefing package for a student competition, this solution combined the functions of an envelope, folder and loose leaf instruction sheets into one item. Tear-off strips top and bottom converted the envelope to the cover, into which the instruction sheets were stapled. A label with decorative stamp perforations was applied to the envelope.

designed by
williams and phoa, London
designers
Richard Bonner Morgan
Nancy Williams
client
D&AD/Royal Mail
printers
Fernedge
labels: Abacus
perforation
Harrison and Sons
stock
label: Super Flat Sam 80gsm
cover: Chipcote 600 micron
text: Trucote velvet 170gsm

D&AD

89

student awards scheme

van heusen — english collection shirts

deinhard london — lustau almacenista sherr

wiggins teape — conqueror laser

Royal Mail

faber & faber — children's fiction

leeds permanent building society — liquid gold

d&ad tv graphic bursary 1988/89 — focus

in association with primesight — **the designers & art directors association's education programme**

150 The aim of this self promotional brochure was to reflect, as accurately as possible, the unique aspect and quality of the original work that was represented. In order to do so, many techniques were used. These included die-cutting and creasing to recreate a three-dimensional pack; die-cutting to imply three coordinated letter heads, and using punched holes and folded paper inserts held together with ribbon to represent a concert programme. In addition the foil blocked covers of the loose leaf binding were blind embossed to accommodate the interscrews which held the pages in place.

designed by
williams and phoa, London
designers
Nancy Williams
Phoa Kia Boon
printers
CTD
stock
cover: pressboard 600 gsm
text: parilux matt - various
weights

OLYMPIA & YORK

Fleecy Underblanket
PURE WOOL PILE

152 This section comprises a comprehensive list of terms and techniques which are either directly or indirectly related to paper. Entries are listed alphabetically and cross-referenced where necessary.

'A' series International ISO range of paper sizes reducing from the largest, AO (841x1189mm), by folding in half to preserve the same proportions at each reduction. See **Sizes of paper**.

Absorbency The degree to which paper takes up contact moisture, measured by a standard test.

Acid-free Free from acid-producing chemicals and, of more concern to fine artists than designers, acid-free papers are more durable and less prone to yellowing than others.

Air-dried Paper dried by a current of warm air after tub sizing.

Air mail Extremely lightweight paper usually below 40gsm, used for stationery and book interleaves. See **Onion skin**.

All-rag paper Paper made from a pulp made of rags. Now also refers to paper made of cotton linter pulp.

Antique A printing paper with a rough finish but good printing surface, valued in book printing for its high volume. Available in laid or woven.

Archival paper A paper with long-lasting qualities, acid-free, usually with good colour retention.

Artists original High-quality paper, often made from a rag or cotton furnish, that simulates handmade paper but is made in a continuous process using a cylinder mould machine.

Art paper and board See **Gloss art paper**.

'B' Series International ISO range of sizes designated for large items (wall charts and posters) and falling between A series sizes: B0 is 1000 x 1414mm. See **Sizes of paper**.

Backing up Printing the reverse side of a sheet already printed.

Bank Lightweight wood-free writing and printing paper, 45-60 gsm, available in tints, for correspondence, copy typing, multi-part sets (NCR).

Banker Style of envelope with an opening on the long edge and a diamond-shape flap. Described as either high-cut or low-cut depending upon the throat.

Base paper Paper before coating, also known as body paper or body stock.

Basis weight The weight of paper in grammes per square metre.

Basket felt Paper with a weave-effect finish, used for heavy manilla papers.

Bible paper A very thin opaque paper for airmail, bibles, diaries, etc.

Blade-coated Refers to the steel blade which levels and controls the china clay coating applied to base paper. See **Gloss art** and **Matt-coated paper.**

Bleached mechanical Paper made of chemically bleached mechanical pulp, sometimes called improved newsprint. Used for inexpensive, one or two-colour magazines.

Bleed Additional margin allowed for pictures that go into the trim area.

Blind embossing Embossing without using ink to create a raised design in paper or card which is visible because of the shadow it casts, white and very dark stocks lessen the shadow effect. Not suitable for items which may be photocopied, faxed or laser printed.

Blistering Heavy coated stocks can blister if printed by heat-set web offset. The heat used to dry the ink causes the moisture in the paper to form blisters.

Block Name for text pages without a cover/before binding.

Blotting Highly absorbent paper used for soaking up excess liquids, e.g. ink.

Board General term for paper above 220 gsm encompassing numerous grades, multi-ply, coated and uncoated.

Body paper See **Base paper**.

Bolt Name given to the folded spine of a folio.

Bond Uncoated paper generally used as writing paper.

Bonding strength The extent to which fibres at the surface of the paper adhere to one another and to the fibres below the surface.

Book paper General term for paper specifically made for book production.

Book jacket General term applied to printed dust cover or wrapper on books, usually a high-quality coated grade.

Brittleness The extent to which paper cracks or breaks when bent or embossed.

Brightness The amount to which a paper reflects white light.

Bristol board High-quality smooth board.

Broke Damaged or defective paper often discarded during manufacture and usually re-pulped.

Broken ream Part of a ream of paper left after use.

Brush-coated Method of coating paper using oscillating brushes.

Bulk The thickness of a paper measured by calliper, volume or ppi.

Bulky mechanical Paperback books, office/store-cash/adding machine paper.

Burst A means to gauge strength of paper.

Bursting Term referring to the separation of perforated sheets.

'C' series ISO envelope sizes, to fit stationery of A series dimensions. See **Sizes of paper**.

Calender Set of rollers through which paper passes under pressure to impart a smooth finish. See **Supercalender**.

Calliper The thickness of a single sheet of paper measured in millimetres, microns or 1/1000 inch. A micron is 1/1000mm.

Carbon paper Base paper usually comprising a thin tissue or other lightweight grade coated on one side with a mixture of carbon black or other colouring agent and a chemical substance which acts as a carrier.

Carbonless paper Comprises a minimum of two sheets of paper: the underside of the top sheet coated with a mix containing colourless dye in minute gelatin capsules, the underneath sheet coated with a mix containing a special dye which turns blue when penetrated by the colourless dye. The application of pressure on the top sheet causes the gelatin capsules to break and the blue dye to appear on the sheet underneath.

Cartridge Printing or drawing paper with good dimensional stability, high opacity and good bulk. Is prone to ink rub, but this can be prevented using inks with a high wax content. Used for drawing paper, envelopes etc.

Case In bookbinding, the covers of a hard-bound book.

Cast-coated papers High-quality printing.

Chain lines The watermark lines which run at right-angles to laid lines on the laid surface of the mould.

Chalking Term used in heat-set web offset when the ink does not key to the surface of the paper and can be removed by rubbing.

Character The distinctive characteristics of a paper such as wove or laid.

Chemical pulp Pulp produced by treating wood with chemicals rather than grinding it mechanically. Chemical pulp contains fewer impurities than mechanical pulp, it is stronger, and produces paper which is less likely to yellow when exposed to light. Papers made of chemically pulped wood are sometimes known as 'wood-free' papers.

Cheque papers Chemically treated security paper, usually to specification, which may contain watermarks and other security features against fraud.

China clay A white refined clay used extensively in loading and coating mixes.

Chipboard A cheap grade of board usually manufactured from lower grades of waste paper and available unlined or lined on one or both sides.

Chromo-coated Usually one-sided coated, high-quality gloss paper or board for proofing, inserts etc.

Cloth lined/centred Paper with a muslin/linen centre or backing used to strengthen. Used for charts, maps, envelopes, identification bags, etc.

Coated paper Paper-coated with china clay or similar materials to give a smooth surface good for halftone reproduction. See **Gloss art** and **Matt coated papers.**

Cockling Wavy edges on paper caused by unstable atmospheric conditions.

Cold pressed (CP) The surface quality of a sheet of paper. See **Not**.

Concertina fold Folded literally like the bellows section of a concertina.

Conditioning Exposure of paper in controlled atmospheric conditions for moisture equilibrium.

Continuous stationery Stationery paper in perforated reel or folded automatic feed.

Copier paper Lightweight grades of paper used in photocopying machines.

Cotton fibre The soft white filaments attached to the seeds of the cotton plant. Cotton fabric is made from the long fibres, leaving behind short fibres, called linters, which can be used for papermaking. Cotton rags can also be turned into pulp for papermaking. See **Rag**.

Copperplate printing Traditional process using a hand-engraved copper plate, which is printed from using the intaglio method. Generally used for invitations and business cards.

Cover paper and boards Used for catalogues, cards, booklets, etc.

Cross direction Across the web, at right-angles to the machine direction.

Crown See **Sizes of paper**.

Curling A curl can be caused by several factors: the difference in structure or coatings from one side to the other, moving it from one atmosphere to another before printing, which may change its moisture content, or, by contact with the process moisture during printing, e.g. during offset printing.

Custom-making Paper made specially to client specifications.

Cut size paper Small cut sizes for office stationery use.

Cylinder-mould The type of papermaking machine most commonly used today in the production of mould-made papers.

Dandy roll Large cylindrical roller used on a Fourdrinier machine which impresses the watermark on to the paper.

Debossing See **Embossing**.

Deckle edge The wavy, feathered edges of a sheet of handmade or mould-made paper. Handmade paper has four deckle edges; mould-made has two.

Die stamping This process is similar to embossing in that a femal die is used

into which the paper is pressed. In this case the recess of the die is coated with either oil or water-based inks. Metallic inks are sometimes polished by a second hit without ink. Not recommended for laminated, varnished or cast coated stocks. Traditionally used for crests and logos.

Dimensional stability The dimensional stability of a paper is the percentage of elongation or shrinkage caused by a given change in the relative humidity or moisture content in the air. It is a measure of the paper's tendency to misregister.

Discolouration Most papers tend to yellow as they age, particularly in a polluted atmosphere. Papers made from mechanically pulped wood will yellow much more quickly and easily than those made of chemically pulped wood (wood-free). Cheap, coloured papers will fade in sunlight; more expensive ones may contain colouring agents resistant to this.

Dot gain When halftones are printed, the dot on the paper will be bigger than the dot on the printing plate or screen. The amount by which is it bigger is the dot gain, and is dependent on factors such as the surface of the paper, the pressure used and the type of ink.

Double-coated Paper which has been passed through the coater twice.

DPI Dot per inch - used to describe fineness of a printer's screen - usually from 150 to 400DPI.

Drawing papers and boards High-quality papers, either handmade or mould-made, often tub-sized and with an all-rag furnish.

Duplex papers and boards Two qualities or colours combined on the paper machine.

Duplicating papers Unsized and semi-sized papers with a built-in quick-drying facility for use in the duplicating process.

Embossing Creating a raised surface pattern in paper or card by pressing it between a male and female metal die. For simple designs the die can be photo-engraved; more complex patterns have to be engraved by hand, which is more expensive. To prevent the paper splitting a non-coated stock with long or random fibres should be used. If the image is sunk into the page it can be described as debossed. See **Blind embossing.**

Enamel paper High gloss-coated on one side.

Endpaper Strong paper used for securing the body of a book to its case.

Engine sized Chemicals added during pulp preparation to aid surface ink resistance.

Environmentally friendly (See **Recycled**) A paper may be environmentally friendly for any/all of the following reasons:
- There is a policy of re-planting to replace those cut down to be pulped.
- No chlorine is used in the bleaching process. Bleaching pulp with chlorine results in toxic effluents.
- High straw content, therefore less wood pulp needed.
- The papermaking process used is itself environmentally friendly - for instance, the mill uses as little energy as possible, and minimises or cleans the effluents it releases into the environment.

Esparto Type of grass from North Africa with good papermaking fibre properties for smoothness in writing and printing papers.

Ex merchant stock Papers obtained direct from a merchant's warehouse.

Ex mill stock Papers ordered through a merchant for delivery from mill stock.

154

Fastness Resistance of colour to fading.

Felt mark The rough surface of paper, dried naturally covered by felt.

Fibres The basic structural material in all sheets of paper. Most papers contain wood fibres, but fibres suitable for papermaking can be extracted from cotton, linen, jute, kozo, gampi, manila and many other materials. The longer the fibres, the stronger the paper.

Fillers Substances which are added to the pulp to make a harder, more opaque paper surface.

Fine papers High-quality papers.

Finish A general term for the surface characteristics of papers and boards.

Finishing Processes that the printed sheet goes through in order to produce the final item, e.g. creasing, die-cutting, binding etc. Also, in paper making this term refers to the practices of drying, sizing and looking over sheets of paper after the papermaking processes are completed.

Flexographic Cost-effective printing technique used on rotary-fed production.

Fluorescent paper Dyed or coated with fluorescent pigments activated by UV light to glow brightly.

Foam-centred board Display boards for advertising, promotions etc.

Foil blocking Technique of applying a thin layer of metal or foil to the surface of paper using a metal block, heat and pressure. It is the only way to achieve a truly metallic look with a smooth, shiny surface. Also provides an opaque media when blocking light colours onto dark, or flat colour onto flecked stock.

Foil-lined boards Box making, labels, wrappers especially for food.

Foil papers and boards Papers and boards with a metallic laminated surface.

Folding boxboard White lined boards made from a top-quality furnish, coated, impregnated or laminated with exceptional scoring and folding properties.

Folio In book production, a sheet of paper which is folded to form pages, always comprising multiples of 4. Also refers to pages number. See **Signature**.

Foolscap See **Sizes of paper**.

Formation The fibre distribution in a sheet of paper as it appears when held up to the light.

French folds/binding Term used to describe concertina-folded pages which are bound at the spine.

Furnish The mixture of pulp and additives from which a paper is made.

Fourdrinier The name of a type of paper machine in which paper is made at high speed in a continuous web.

Galley proof Proof of setting before being made into pages, rarely used.

Gampi Used for papermaking in Japan, its thin, glossy fibres result in translucent papers which are very tough.

Gate fold Describes pages which fold inward from a central page.

Ghosting Normally seen when solids are printed with white out areas that appear as ghost images within the solid print.

Glacine Transparent paper used for window envelopes, photo bags, interleaving books, sweet packaging, etc. Is available embossed with intricate patterns and in rich colours.

Glazing The process of smoothing a paper surface, usually by running dried sheets through steel rollers or between polished zinc plates.

Gloss The light reflectiveness of the surface of a sheet of paper; a shiny or lustrous appearance.

Gloss art papers These are highly calendered china clay or chalk-coated papers, with the following properties:
- provide the highest-quality reproduction in terms of detail/definition
- the ink sits on top of the paper allowing it to dry quickly
- minimal dot distortion/dot gain
- can reproduce fine screens up to 400 dpi
- inks often appear matt against the paper surface
- opacity and bulk not as good as matt paper because of calendering.

Gloss ghosting Effect caused by a combination of the paper quality and the amount of ink and varnish being carried, which can cause a yellow ghosting on the paper white areas of the reverse side to a dense printed image.

Grain The alignment of fibres in machine or mould-made paper, sometimes called machine direction. Long grain or grain means that the fibres run parallel to the longest side of a sheet; short grain, that they run parallel to the shortest side. Handmade paper has no grain as the fibres are distributed randomly. The grain of a machine or mould-made paper results in the following properties:
- The paper tears more easily along the grain
- It folds more easily and sharply along the grain: consequently folds should be aligned along the grain
- It is stronger and stiffer across the grain
- It expands or contracts across the grain - consequently, when printing, the grain should run across the machine
The following are ways of assessing the grain direction in a paper:
- Look at the packet label of the unprinted paper; in the UK the second dimension of the sheet size indicates the grain direction. e.g. 450 x 640mm is long grain; 640 x 450mm is short grain
- Slowly tear the paper in one direction, then again at right-angles. The straightest tear will be the one in the grain direction
- Wet a sample of the paper. The axis of curl is in the grain direction
- For board; flex a square piece in both directions. The stiffest will be at right angles to the grain direction.

Grammage (gsm/gm2) The weight of a single one metre square sheet of a paper. It is expressed in grams per square metre (gsm or gm2).

Greaseproof Translucent paper, with a high resistance to penetration by grease or fats, produced by prolonged heating in the pulp stage.

Greyboard Board made entirely from waste paper; used in bookbinding and packaging.

Gripper edge Leading edge of paper as it passes though a printing press.

Gripper margin Unprintable blank edge of paper which is held by the grippers which control the flow of the sheet as it passes though the printing press.

Gummed papers Base papers web-coated with water-based adhesive.

Gusset pocket An open-end envelope with expandable sides.

Gutter The blank space or printed area between pages which runs into the binding.

gm2/gsm Grams per square metre - see **Grammage**.

Handmade Paper made by hand.

Heat-sealed Paper coated with an adhesive material that is activated by the application of heat.

Hickeys In offset-lithography, spots or imperfections in the printing due to such things as dried ink skin, paper particles, etc.

Hinges The sections of a cover adjoining the spine which are glued to the book block in the binding process.

Hot pressed (HP) Handmade or mould-made paper with a smooth surface achieved by passing sheets through hot, heavy metal plates or rollers.

Hygroscopic Tends to absorb moisture from the air.

Imitation art Paper highly loaded with china clay and gloss finish to give the appearance of coated art.

Imperial See **Sizes of paper**.

Imposition The way in which pages are arranged so that after printing and folding they are in the correct order.

Index board Strong board usually made from chemical wood-pulp, having a smooth surface and being hard sized, for index cards and stationery.

India paper Very thin, high-quality, opaque rag paper often used for bibles.

Ink jet paper Printing paper produced specifically for use with the ink jet printing process.

Ink rub Problem which occurs when the ink has not adhered firmly to the surface of the paper.

In line Describes any process, e.g. printing, drying, UV varnish, which is part of a single pass through a printing machine.

Intaglio Printing process which uses paper and pressure process to draw the ink from the recesses in an engraved plate.

Interleaves Blank sheets or pages used to protect illustrations.

ISO sizes Formerly DIN sizes. International range of paper and envelope sizes, comprising A series, B series and C series. See **Sizes of paper**.

Ivory board Used for visiting cards, high-quality notices, tickets and menus.

Kozo Used for papermaking in Japan. Its long fibres result in very durable papers which retain their strength even when folded or crumpled.

Kraft Glazed manila paper used for wrapping purposes with a high mechanical strength. Also produced in white, called bleached kraft.

Label paper Wide range of paper grades coated on one side with adhesive.

Laid paper Paper that is made on a laid mould (as opposed to a wove mould). If laid paper is held up to the light, closely spaced parallel lines can be seen. It is customary for these laid lines to run across the page's width and the chain lines from head to foot.

Lamination Bonding two sheets, either of the same or differing materials to stiffen or protect e.g paper to board, board to matt/gloss coating.

Lay Orientation of a sheet of paper through the printing press.

Laydown Indication of the position of an artwork on a sheet of paper.

Leaf fibre Leaf fibres, such as manila, can be used for making paper. However, they tend to be short fibres, resulting in weaker papers.

Letterpress A relief form of printing, which takes the impression from a block or typeset metal, using pressure.

Litho Abbreviation. See **Offset litho.**

Linen Linen, which has long fibres, can be used to produce strong, fine papers. Produces high-quality stationery paper.

Linters See **Cotton fibre**.

Loading China clay, chalk and other minerals mixed in with pulp.

Long grain See **Grain**

Machine-coated Coating applied to base paper while on papermaking machine.

Machine glazed Gloss finish on one side achieved by drying against large-diameter heated cylinder.

Making order Minimum quantity for special making of paper.

Manifold paper Lightweight bank paper, less than 44 gsm.

Manila paper Strong paper for envelopes and files, formerly made from hemp.

Matt-coated papers Papers with a matt coating of china clay or chalk, between 12 and 22 gsm. Matt-coated papers have the following properties:
- good opacity and bulk
- better durability than art papers
- the non-reflective surface enhances legibility of type
- good for high-resolution images
- will take gloss varnish
- prone to ink rub because of unevenness of surface
- the porous surface sometimes absorbs ink unevenly.

Matt uncoated papers These are made from chemically processed wood-pulp, and have the following properties:
- high opacity and bulk
- more durable than coated papers
- do not crack along fold lines
- can have problems with set off/ink rub
- slight dot gain because of absorbency
- colours look flatter than on coated stock
- do not take varnish well
- sometimes require opaque inks
- take embossing and watermarks well
- maximum screen commonly used 150 DPI
- good for reproducing illustrations.

M weight Term used in the US for the weight of 1,000 sheets of any given paper size.

Machine direction See **Grain**.

Mechanical wood pulp Pulp produced mechanically, by grinding the wood, rather than by treating it with chemicals. The term is also used to describe paper made of this pulp. Mechanical pulp is weaker than chemical pulp, and results in paper which is more likely to yellow if exposed to light. Gives cheap, opaque papers used for newspaper, paperback books etc.

MF Machine-finished: smooth surface obtained by on-machine calendering.

Millpack A term used for 100-125 sheets of paper. See **Volume/quantity of paper.**

Mitsumata Used for papermaking in Japan, its long fibres result in strong, glossy papers which are naturally insect resistant.

Moisture content Moisture in paper, expressed as a percentage of weight.

Mould-made Paper made on cylinder-mould machine imitating handmade.

NAPM National Association of Paper Merchants.

Newsprint The cheapest printing paper, used to make newspapers. Has good

opacity and bulk, but a poor surface and low brightness. Entirely made of mechanical pulp, it discolours easily. Unsuitable for screens finer than 100 DPI.
NCR No carbon required. See **Carbonless paper**.
Not The slightly rough, unglazed surface of a paper (abbreviation of 'not hot pressed'). Produced when a handmade or mould-made paper is repressed without felts. This gives a surface finish between rough and hot-pressed.

OCR paper High-quality wood-free bond for optical character recognition.
Offset litho printing Offsets the right reading image from a flat, sensitised plate on to a blanket cylinder before transferring to the paper.Process which uses the property of oil on water, not mixing. See **Sheet-fed** and **Web printing**.
One-sided art High-quality paper coated on one side for book jacket covers.
Onion skin Extremely lightweight paper with a cockle finish. See **Air mail**.
Opacity The extent to which printing on the reverse of a sheet of paper shows through - the more opaque the paper is, the less likely it is that the printing will show through.
Optical brightener Dye used to brighten paper by fluorescence to UV.
Ozalid proof Dye-line print taken from film before printing plates are made. Used as cheap alternative to printed proofs or to check corrections have been made correctly.

PAA Paper Agents Association.
Pallet Wood base, holding specific quantity of paper.
Particle gummed paper Base paper coated with remoisturable adhesive in small particles to ensure paper remains flat.
Part mechanical Paper containing up to 50% of mechanical pulp.
Paste board Used for high-quality heavyweight boxes for cosmetics and confectionery.
PH The pH value is a measure of the strength of the acidity or alkalinity of a paper. A pH of 0 is very acid, 14 is very alkaline, 7 is neutral.
Perfect binding Sections of a book are milled off along the bolt then notched and glued together before drawing on the cover. Pages cannot be opened out flat and can only be used satisfactorily on spines over 3mm thick.
Photographic proof Coloured proof made from film separations such as chromalin matchprint, Fuji Color Art, etc.
Picking The release of surface fibres from paper during printing.
PIRA Printing Industries Research Association.
Platesinking Debossing a sunken area on a page or cover to hold a tipped-in picture or label.
Ply A layer of paper or board, joined to others for strength. The resulting paper or board will be described as 2 ply, 3 ply etc depending on the number of layers.
Pocket Envelope style with one side or centre seam, a bottom flap and opening on the short side.
PPA Periodical Publishers Association.
Ppi Pages per inch - term used in US to specify paper thickness.
PPIC Pulp and Paper Information Centre.
Presspahn Glazed board, extra hard-rolled and often friction-glazed, is extremely durable and moisture-resistant. Originally used for industrial applications, but useful for folders and covers.

Press proofs In colour reproduction, a proof of a colour subject on a printing press, in advance of the production run.
Progressive proofs (progs) Proofs made from the separate plates in colour process work, showing the sequence of printing and the result after each additional colour has been applied; helps identify problems.
Proof Limited print run, taken from printing plates, usually on a flat-bed press, to enable the work to be checked before printing.
Pulp The main ingredient in the papermaking process, usually made from processed wood, cotton linters or rags.

Quire A British term for 25 sheets of paper, a twentieth part of a ream.
See **Volume/quantity of paper**.

Rag Cotton rag used as the principal raw material in the papermaking process. 'Rag content' describes the amount of cotton fibre relative to the total amount of material used in the pulp. The term is not widely used now, or is a misnomer, as more and more high-quality paper is made not from rag but from linters.
See **Cotton**.
Rattle The sound produced by shaking a piece of paper. In general, the harder the rattle, the better the quality - although there are exceptions.
Ream Traditionally 480 sheets (equal to 20 quires of 24 sheets). Now taken to refer to 500 sheets. See **Volume/quantity of paper**.
Recycled (see **Environmentally friendly)** 'Recycled' is a vague term used to describe a wide variety of types of paper. Very few papers are made entirely from recycled fibres - usually a proportion of virgin fibres are added for strength, this proportion varies from paper to paper. The 'recycled' content of a paper may include any of the following:
- pulp left over from the previous batch of papermaking
- pulp made from clean off-cuts from virgin sheets, known as 'broke'
- pulp made from paper which has been printed on and used, then collected, sorted and re-pulped. It is often assumed that this sort of 'post-consumer waste' is the basic ingredient of all recycled papers, whereas some recycled papers, especially those which look very 'clean', have a very low post-consumer waste content.
The environmental reasons for using recycled paper include the following:
- it uses half the energy and one third of the water of virgin paper
- fewer chemicals are used, resulting in less effluent
- paper and board form about a half of all domestic waste - disposing of our waste is becoming increasingly expensive and difficult.
Reel A continuous length of paper wound on a core irrespective of diameter, width or weight.
Repro paper Paper with a hard sized coating and good absorbency character.
Retree Paper with small imperfections at reduced price.
Ribbed Paper finish traditionally used for heavyweight manila papers.
Roll coating applied by rollers, usually on machine.
Rough A term used to describe the surface texture of a sheet of handmade or mould-made paper when it is left to dry naturally.
Rub Can occur on matt coated paper when the peaks on the surface literally get rubbed off or act as an abrasive and remove the print surface from an adjacent sheet.

Saddle wire stitched Correct term for binding using wire; has the appearance of staples. Available in steel and copper, can be formed into loops on the spine side for use in ring binders.

Satin papers See **Silk papers**.

SC Abbreviation of supercalendered. See **Calendered**.

Section See **Folio**.

Security paper Paper with features which make counterfeiting difficult.

Self-adhesive paper Paper with a self-adhesive coating protected by laminate on one side and a good surface suitable for printing on the other.

Self copy See **Carbonless**.

Self cover Cover using same paper as text pages.

Set off Image from the wet side of the sheet marking the reverse side of the sheet above. Anti-set-off spray commonly is used to help prevent this.

Sheet Refers to a sheet of papers. The term 'good sheet' refers to a sheet which prints well.

Sheet-fed printing Describes printing onto flat sheets as opposed to web which is onto a reel. Is generally considered to be of higher quality than web printing because of the greater control of register.

Short grain Paper in which the grain is parallel to the shorter edge of the sheet.

Shoulder Top of the side flap on a wallet envelope. A critical design aspect for most inserting machines.

Show-through The extent to which the image printed on one side of the paper is evident on the reverse.

Signature A printed sheet of paper that on folding becomes a section of a book. Also refers to the sheet once folded. See **Folio**.

Silk papers These fall between matt and gloss-coated papers and have some of the advantages of both, such as:
- medium opacity and bulk
- can give high-quality reproduction, with good definition of details
- text printed on these papers reads well due to the low reflectivity of the surface.

Silkscreen printing In addition to paper, can be used to print a wide variety of materials which would not go through the rollers of a litho press e.g. card, plastic, fabric, metal. Good for bold designs, blocks of colour; less good for delicate work. Can be problematic for very light papers (which will shrink after printing) and uncoated stocks (which may take a long time to dry).

Singer sewn Industrial version of domestic sewing machine stitching, used for binding and increasingly difficult to obtain. Usually stitches go though the book front but can, with skilled finishing, run along the spine.

Sizing Treatment of papers during manufacture to make them less absorbent/more water-resistant.

Sizes of paper The ISO (International Organisation for Standardisation) series of paper measurements is the only system of measurement used in the machine-made paper trade, though its three denominations, A, B and C, are not necessarily applicable to newspapers , books or some stationery items. The A series is used to denote paper sizes for general printing matter, B is primarily for posters and wall charts and C is specifically for envelopes. Dimensions in millimetres:

A Series
A0 841 x 1,189 **A1** 594 x 841 **A2** 420 x 594 **A3** 297 x 420 **A4** 210 x 297 **A5** 148 x 210 **A6** 105 x 148 **A7** 74 x 105 **A8** 55 x 74 **A9** 37 x 55 **A10** 28 x 37 **4A0** 1,682 x 2,378 **2A0** 1,189 x 1,681

B Series
Trimmed sizes falling between A sizes designed for large items, for instance posters.
B0 1,000 x 1,414 **B1** 707 x 1,000 **B2** 500 x 707 **B3** 353 x 500 **B4** 250 x 353 **B5** 176 x 250 **4B** 2,000 x 2,828 **2B** 1,414 x 2,000

C Series
Envelopes and folders to take A series contents.
C0 917 x 1297 **C1** 648 x 917 **C2** 458 x 648 **C3** 324 x 458 **C4** 229 x 324 **C5** 162 x 229 **C6** 114 x 162 **C7/6** 81 x 162 **C7** 81 x 114 **DL** 110 x 220

ISO Series untrimmed stock sizes
The untrimmed paper sizes of the ISO A series which are intended to be trimmed to A sizes after printing are made in the following additional denominations, used mainly in machine-made paper designations.
The RA series (addition of an R to the A series) is for non-bled printing and includes approximately an extra 10-20mm onto the A size which is trimmed off after printing. The SRA series (addition of an SR to the A series) is used when printed work is bled off the edge of trimmed size and an extra 30-40mm is allowed on the A size for trimming after printing is completed. e.g.
A2 420 x 594 **RA2** 430 x 610 **SRA2** 450 x 640

Imperial sizes
Imperial measurements were used in Britain from 1836 until metrication. The picturesque names given to the sheet sizes were derived from the watermarks used by the old mills - different mills made different sizes of paper. Although machine-made paper is now sold in metric measurements, some of the more common Imperial terms, such as those listed below, are still referred to especially for handmade paper.
Crown 508 x 381 **Double crown** 508 x 762 **Quad crown** 762 x 1016 **Imperial** 762 x 559 **Half imperial** 381 x 559 **Double imperial** 762 x 1118 **Foolscap** 343 x 432 **Double foolscap** 432 x 686 **Quad foolscap** 686 x 864
The name for this paper derives from the fact that it used to have a watermark of a court jester's hat.

Smoothness The smoothness of a paper is essentially the flatness of its surface. It is not the same as 'gloss', which is an optical property.

Spread Describes two adjacent pages when opened out flat.

Straw For environmental reasons, straw is being used as an alternative to wood fibre in papermaking, although not yet on a large scale.

Stock A term loosely applied to papermaking material in all its stages but also refers to the wet pulp before it is fed on to the paper machine.

Substance Weight of paper and board. See **gsm**.

Supercalender Off machine calender stack of alternate hard and soft rolls to impart smoothness and gloss. See **Calender**.

Surface finish The surface character of a sheet of paper, for instance, CP, HP, Not, burnished, hammered, etc.

Synthetic papers Papers made from synthetic material rather than natural.

Texture The rough surface of a paper. Can be a natural result of pulp and processing or a contrived impression.

Thermography Technique of sprinkling resin on to wet ink to produce a raised,

158

glossy surface after heating. Often used for logos on letterheads, it gives an effect rather like die stamping, but is cheaper.

Thickness of paper See **Calliper**.

Thread sewing Signatures of a book are sewn together before binding.in 8,16 and sometimes 32. This enables pages to be opened out flat.

Three-hole sewings Traditional alternative to saddle wire stitching, using a single thread in a figure-of-eight, which is increasingly difficult to obtain.

Throat Gap between the scoreline and back flap of a wallet envelope. A critical design aspect for most inserting machines.

Thumb cut Shape cut from a pocket or wallet to facilitate access to contents.

Ticket board Another name for pasteboard, although coated board can be included in this grade.

Tipping-in Sticking with adhesive, usually an illustration or photograph, onto a page, often made of a different stock or material.

Tissue paper Very thin, lightweight paper for interleaving and wrapping.

Tooth Characteristic, rough texture of a paper surface.

Top side Opposite of wire side, the side of paper away from the wire during manufacture.

Tracking Relative positions of pages that are inked in the cylinder rotation direction and follow one behind the other. Therefore images in the same track cannot be treated separately in terms of ink feed.

Triplex board Board made from three layers or lined on both sides.

Trim Area surrounding the page or image area.

Twin wire Papers and boards made from two separate webs on a twin wire paper machine.

Two-sidedness Term given to paper or board which exhibits different surface characteristics on either side of the sheet.

um Abbreviation of micron, 1/1000mm, used as a measurement of the thickness of a sheet of paper.

Uncoated mechanical sc A smooth, supercalendered stock providing good halftone reproduction. A lightweight, cheap alternative to coated paper.

Uncoated papers See **Matt uncoated papers**.

UV varnish Matt or gloss protective coating which is harden using ultra-violet light. Can be prone to cracking along the spine.

Vellum Paper made from the inner side of calfskin. The term is also used to describe papers made from other materials which imitate real vellum.

Velvet papers See **Silk papers**.

Volume Thickness of paper expressed as volume for book production.

Volume/quantity of paper
- Ream - 500 sheets, although traditionally it was 480
- Quire - 25 sheets
- Millpack - 100 to 125 sheets

Virgin fibre Fibre used for the first time to make paper (i.e. not recycled).

Wallet Envelope style with two side seams and the opening on the long edge.

Watermark A translucent design in a sheet of paper that can be seen when it is held up to the light. Watermarks are made by incorporating a raised device into the mould when the paper is made so that that part of the paper is thinner and therefore translucent. Most watermarks are linear designs, but some - chiaroscuro watermarks - are made by putting a sculptured device into the mould to produce results such as the Queen's head found on British bank notes. Watermarks are generally read from the right side of the paper.

Web The reel of wound paper in its entire width at the end of a paper machine prior to splitting into smaller rolls or cutting into sheets. Also known as mother roll.

Web offset A form of offset litho, this process prints and sometimes finishes in one continuous pass onto a web of paper. When heat is used to facilitate finishing it is called Heat set. This can lead to the subsequent expansions of pages when atmospheric moisture is absorbed. When combined with sheet fed covers the Web text pages often protrude after trimming. It is generally used for high volume work such as magazines and though it is poorly perceived, dramatic improvements in quality have been made in recent years.

Weight Weight or grammage of a sheet of paper normally expressed in gsm.

Window Aperture in envelope usually covered with glacine paper.

Wireside/wiremark The surface of the pulp in contact with the mesh during papermaking.

Wood-free Papers which are made of chemically pulped wood (as opposed to mechanically pulped) are sometimes referred to as 'wood-free' papers.

Wood pulp Wood pulp is made by chemically or mechanically processing wood. Nowadays the majority of papers are made from wood pulp rather than, for instance, cotton/rag pulp.

Work and tumble To print one side of a sheet of paper, then turn the sheet over from gripper to back using the same side guide and plate to print the second side.

Work and turn To print one side of a sheet of paper, then turn the sheet over from left to right and print the second side using the same plate. The same gripper and lay edge are used for printing both sides.

Wove papers Papers made in wove moulds, as opposed to laid moulds. In a wove mould the covering screen is made of woven wire, similar to the warp and weft in cloth, and the resulting paper has no obvious markings.

Wrap-round cover Describes a cover which is not physically attached to the pages beneath, but held in place by the friction caused by 'wrapping' it round.

The author would like to thank the following companies for their contribution to this book. Acknowledgments to:
Art-O-Matic
Baddeley Brothers (London) Limited
British Printing Industries Federation
R K Burt & Co Ltd
CTD Printers Ltd
Estamp Publishing
Paper Power (creative paper engineering)
St Ives plc

A & A Vacuum Packing, **121**
Abacus, **148**
acid etching, **115**
Adams, Sean, **18**
aeroply, birch-faced, **126**
aircraft plywood, **125**
Albany Packaging, **71**
Allman Associates, **21**
alternative materials, **115-28**
  cotton, **116**
  metal, **117-18**
  perspex, **119-20**
  plastic, **121**
  PVC, **122**
  rag, **124**
  wood, **125-8**
  aluminium, **117**
Anderson Fraser, **141**
Arches Velin, **49**
Area, **26, 71, 72, 119, 121**
Art-O-Matic, **58, 71, 108, 119, 121, 122, 146**
artwork, paper as, **16-17**
Asahi Seihan Printing, **46**
Axis, **91**

B & H Group, **56**
Baddeley Brothers, **52**
Bahruth, Reinbek, **48**
Baskerville typeface, **49**
Bateson, John, **40, 137**
Bell, Nick, **126, 140**
Benoit Jacques, **134**
Berol, **102**
Beuys, Joseph, **140**
BFS, **65**
binding, **64, 65-71**
birch-faced aeroply, **126**
Blenheim Group, **70**
Bonner Morgan, Richard, **108, 148**
bookbinders' string, waxed, **140**
Boom, Irma, **47, 66**
Booth, David, **32, 85**
Boots Company, **85**
bracken, **28**
Bradforth, Paul, **37**
Bradley, Chris, **40**
British Rail, **40**
British Rail Parcels Group, **137**
Bticino, **122**
bubble wrap, **132, 137**
Bull, John, **92, 135**
Bull Rodger, **21, 37, 59, 92, 135**
Butlers Wharf, **68**

Caddy, Adrian, **32, 52**
Cape, Jonathan, **105**
cardboard, corrugated, **137, 140**

cardboard engineering, **97**
Carrow, Peter, **68**
Carter, Philip, **16**
Carter Wong, **16**
cartridge paper, **135**
Caslon typeface, **49**
cast iron, **111**
CGS, **86**
Charlton (Chrissie) & Company, **65**
Chater Press, **72, 94**
Chelsea Flower Show, **25**
Chipcote, **148**
Christie, Agatha, **82**
clean, **136**
clocks, **108**
cloth, **115**
cotton, **116**
coated carton board, **108**
coated cartridge paper, **135**
coffee-percolator paper, **66**
collage, **14**
Colourstyle, **106**
Comme des Garcons, **118**
concertina fold, **153**
concertinas, **70**
conditioning, **153**
Consort Royal Silk, **20**
Consort Royal Supreme Matt, **70, 117, 126**
Consort Royal Supreme Silk, **137**
Continental Bournique, **39**
Cook, Jonathan, **21, 37**
corrugated cardboard, **137, 140**
cotton fibre, **29, 116**
Craft B flute, **108**
Croxley Script, **59**
CTD, **68, 70, 141, 144, 150**
cutting and folding, **63, 72-3**

Davis, Imogen, **104**
debossing, **35**
Delaney (Brian) Design Associates, **13, 29**
Denny, Michael, **40, 137**
Design and Art Direction (D&AD), **16, 94, 148**
Dew, Shaun, **141**
die-cutting, **63, 74-91**
die-stamping, **36, 52**
DinDisc, **79**
Dinnis, Rachael, **40**
Dot For Dot, **72, 119**
drafting film, **58, 140**
draw film, **125**
Drukkerij Rosbeek, **22, 47, 66**
Duckworth, Bruce, **94**
Duffin Containers, **108**
Dunbar, Karin, **72, 94**

Dyverse, **115**

'E' flute corrugated, **101**
Earthlife, **28**
Elephant-hide, white, **68**
embossing, **35-6, 37-44**
environmentally friendly, **14-15**
expandable corrugated board, **117**

Fabriano Designo, **147**
Fabriano Rosaspina bianco, **136**
Face, **147**
Face Photosetting, **88**
Facsimile Printing Company, **60**
Fell Ribbon and Impact Printing, **108**
Fernedge, **148**
First Impression, **24**
Five Oaks Investments, **122**
flute board, **137**
Foggo, Peter, **144**
foil blocking, **36, 47**
folding, **92-3**
  cutting and folding, **63, 72-3**
French folds, **22**
Frost, Vince, **90**
Fuji Paper Enterprise Association, **43**
Fulmar Colour Printing, **40, 122**

Gallardo, Cara, **26, 71, 72, 119, 121**
Galliano, John, **72, 121**
GB Flannel, **52**
GF Smith Colour plan, **92**
Giant, **58, 125**
Gibbons, Steve, **122**
Gill (Nicholas) Associates, **17**
Gill typeface, **49**
glass, **142**
Goldsmiths Gallery, **32**
Goode, Nigel, **106**
graphic recycling, **13, 14, 28-32**
Greiman (April) Incorporated, **18**
Grinter, Laurence, **37, 59, 135**
Guinan (Sarah) Associates, **65**

Hall, Janine, **104**
Halpin Grey Vermeir, **112**
Harden, Richard, **121**
Harden (Richard) Printing, **26**
Harrison and Sons, **148**
Haymar Acrylic, **119**
Heard, Laura, **25, 146**
Hector Martin, **54**
Herron, Alan, **58**
Hey, Martyn, **58**
Hillman, David, **101**
Hipwell Bookbinders, **60**
House, Keren, **28, 69**

House of Questa Ltd, **82**
Hudspith, Derick, **102**
Humber Contract Furniture, **20**
Huntsman mark resistant, **144, 146**

Ideal Standard, **101**
Igarashi, Takenobu, **74, 91, 111**
Igarashi Studio, **74, 91, 111**
Ikonorex Special Matt Ivory, **104**
Imagination Design and Communication, **32, 52**
Inclusions Florale, **13, 25**
Independent Curators Incorporated, **81**
Indepth, **32**
inks, **35**
  thermochronic, **35, 56**
Inoue Paper, **132**
ISTD Papers, **80**
Italian Ingres Fabriano, **140**
Ito, Makoto, **43**
Ivorex smooth card, **42**

JAC Brilliant Gloss self-adhesive label paper, **59**
Japanese papers, **13**
Jestico & Whiles, **117**

Kaskad Osprey, **54**
Kazu Jewelry Design Studio, **98**
Keaykolour, **24, 56**
Keaykolour Bockingford Not, **108**
Keeble, Chris, **104**
Keeble & Hall, **104**
Kelly, Ben, **79**
Keyworth, Celia, **90**
Kimpton, David, **28**
Knoll International, **86**
Koeweiden Postma, **138**
Konu & Morrow, **146**
Kueh, Albert, **68, 117**
Kusumoto, Takeshi, **132**

laser-cutting, **63, 91, 94, 115**
Laub, Elisabeth, **77**
leaf dishing weights, **140**
Lense tissue, **25**
letterpress, **35, 46, 48-53**
Levett, Chrissy, **65**
Lewis, Mary, **54, 72, 85, 94**
Lewis Moberly, **54, 72, 85, 94**
Linea Legno, **128**
Lippa, Domenic, **20**
Lippa Pearce, **20**
Litho-tech, **32, 68, 117**
Lloyd Loom furniture, **97**
loft insulation foam, **140**
Lyon, Harvey, **60**

160

M & M, **112**
M Plus M Incorporated, **39, 81, 86, 118**
McConnell, John, **88**
McGinn, Michael, **39, 81**
McKenzie, Sarah, **56, 70, 144**
McLoughlin, Martin, **122**
manipulation, **63-94**
  binding, **65-71**
  cutting and folding, **72-3**
  die-cutting, **74-91**
  folding, **92-3**
  laser-cutting, **94**
Mapledon Press, **40**
Martin, Augustus, **30**
Matsumoto, Takaaki, **39, 86, 118**
matt art paper, **21**
matt inks, **35**
Mellotex Matt Ultra White, **17**
Mellotex Smooth Ultra White, **87**
Mellotex Ultra White, **146**
Merlin Reprographics, **32**
metal, **115, 117-18**
Milne (Peter) Furniture Makers, **126**
Minami, Katsuji, **44**
mixed media, **131-50**
Monarch Press, **81**
mounting board, **108**
Muheim, Andrea, **116**
Muheim family, **116**
musical mechanisms, **147**
Mytton, Robert, **70**

N & N, **24**
Nagai, Kazumasa, **38**
Nautilus Press & Paper Mill, **29**
New Order, **78**
Newell, Frances, **102**
Newell and Sorrell, **102**
Nissha Printing Company, **74, 118**
Nogami, Shuichi, **46**
Novak, Michelle, **77**

Odiwe, Romanus, **24**
offset litho, **35, 54-7, 115**
Ohlson, Barbro, **49, 50**
Okumura, Akio, **27, 43, 44, 46, 98-100, 132**
Olympia and York, **25**
Olympia U.S.A., **75**
Osborne, Charles, **42**
Owen, Mark, **24**

packaging, **97-102**
Packaging Create Inc, **27, 43, 44, 46, 98, 100, 132**
paper qualities, **13-15, 18-27**
papier mâché, **106**
Paragon Vintners, **37**

Parilux gloss, **40**
Parilux matt, **17, 40, 68, 144, 150**
The Partners, **28, 68, 69, 80,122, 124, 141**
Pearce, Harry, **20**
Pearce, Jack, **60**
Pearl Dot, **54**
Pelham, David, **105**
Pen Plus Inc, **39**
Pentagram, **78, 84, 88, 90, 101, 105, 142**
Pentonville Rubber, **119**
Perry, Sarah, **137**
perspex, **119-20**
pH, **156**
Philipp, Marco, **116**
Phoa Kia Boon, **17, 42, 70, 87, 108, 144, 147, 150**
Pirtle, Woody, **84**
Planet Display, **124**
plastic, **115, 121**
plywood, **125**
pocket POD, **84**
Polyart, **115**
pop-ups, **97, 104-5**
Pressboard, **80, 150**
Priestman, Paul, **106**
Priestman Associates, **106**
Puff Fairclough, **72**
Purley Press, **80**
PVC, **122**

Radford & Ball, **142**
Rae, Shonagh, **50**
rag, **124**
recycled paper, **13, 14-15**
Reprof ag CH Gurtnellen, **116**
RHS Print Finishers, **108**
Richard de Bas Mill, **13**
Richards, Lucy, **52**
Richardson, Darren, **137**
Rives satin transparent, **21**
Rivoli, **25**
Rivoli Natural, **49**
Rodacote, **70**
Rodger, Paul, **21, 37, 59, 92**
Rollinson, Mark, **58**
Ross, Andrew, **60**
Roughton and Fenton, **68**
Roundel Design Group, **40, 137**
Royal College of Art, **28**
Royal Mail, **16, 82, 148**
rubber bands, **65, 119**
Rushworth, John, **90, 142**

Sandy Alexander Inc, **77**
Sasago, Yukimi, **91**
Saunders Manufacturing, **118**

Saville, Peter, **78, 79**
Scrimgeour, Lucilla, **85**
sculpture, **97, 111-12**
sealing-wax, **134**
Seibu, **100**
Shakespear, Lorenzo, **142**
Sharples, Sue, **37**
Signo, **122, 128**
Silk Pearce, **60**
silkscreen, **35, 58, 115**
Simulator, **126**
Smith, Neil, **58**
Smith, Nigel, **87**
Smith, Richard, **26, 71, 72, 119, 121**
Snape, John, **37**
Somerset White Satin, **49, 50**
Somerset White Textured, **25**
Sorrell, John, **102**
Southbank Offset, **87**
Southern California Institute
of Architecture, **18**
Speckletone recycled paper, **30**
Sporre, Yvonne, **26, 71, 119**
steel rods, nuts and washers, **126**
strawboard, **30**
string, **134**
  waxed bookbinders, **140**
Stuart, David, **68, 124**
Super Exelda, **49**
Super Flat Sam labels, **148**
surface effects, **35-60**
  embossing, **37-44**
  foil blocking, **47**
  letterpress, **46, 48-53**
  offset litho, **54-7**
  silkscreen, **58**

tipping-in, **59-60**
Taihei Printing, **99**
Talking Europe, **59**
Tanaka, Mikito, **99**
Tatsuno, Koji, **26, 71, 119**
Taylor Bloxham, **104**
Taylor, Stephen A, **136**
terms and techniques, **152**
thermochronic ink, **35, 56**
thermography, **36**
Thomas, Andrew, **82**
three dimensions, **97-112**
  packaging, **97-102**
  pop-ups, **104-5**
  sculpture, **111-12**
  tipping-in, **59-60**
Toller (Fred) Associates, **75**
TQ, **125**
tracing paper, **21**
Transport Design Consortium, **40**
Trickett and Webb, **30, 82**

Triggs, Nina, **92**
Trucote velvet, **148**
Tscherny, Carla, **77**
Tscherny (George) Incorporated, **77**
Tullich Lodge Hotel, **52**
Tyvek, **115**

Una, **93**
Unchino, **99**
uncoated cartridge paper, **135**
Uno drafting film, **140**

Van Driel, Jenni, 22
Veal, Judy, **54**
vellum, **159**
verdigris, **115**
Vermeir, Pierre, **112**
Vitesse Printing, **20**
Vylene, **115**

Waibl, Heinz, **122, 128**
Warner-Chappell Music, **78**
Washi paper, **111**
watermarks, **13**
waxed bookbinders' string, **140**
Webb-Jenkins, Tim, **70**
Wickens, Brett, **78**
Wiese, BK, **48**
Wiese, Bruno and Ruth, **48**
Wiggins Teape Countryside, **60**
Wiggins Teape Opal, **60**
Wiggins Teape Speckletone, **24**
Williams, Nancy, **25, 68, 101,117, 147, 148, 150**
williams and phoa, **17, 25, 42, 56, 68, 70, 87, 108, 117, 144, 146, 147, 148, 150**
Williamson, **84**
Willis, Jeff, **29**
Wong, Philip, **16**
Wood, **125-8**
Wood, Marc, **78**

Yaka Paper Manufacture, **27**
Yamada Shomei Lighting, **111**
Yeats, W.B., **140**

Zanders T2000, **20**
Zeta matt, **42**